THE POWER OF
FOOD PREP

Take the Stress Out of Meal Planning
with the Gourmet Done Skinny Method

Catherine,
Thanks for
making me beautiful!
Love your work!

Amy

AMY LAWRENCE

Bonus

Because there is so much about food prep I couldn't include in the book, I've created a special bonus page for you on my website.

Here's what you'll receive:

- A comprehensive list of items to stock in your kitchen, from dry pantry to freezer and refrigerator
- Links to more of my quick and easy meals that work well for food prep
- A discount on my Food Prep for Foodies membership, a group where I go live and show you how I food prep using the Gourmet Done Skinny Meal Method, give you meal plan ideas, and more
- My resource page with links to my equipment

To get your free bonus, sign up at:
Gourmetdoneskinny.com/power-of-food-prep-bonus-form

For Susan, who encouraged me to write this book and showed me what a true friend is during the most difficult time in my life.

iv

Praise for Amy Lawrence

"I love Amy's approach to food prep; it makes planning meals so much less stressful, whether you're trying to get dinner on the table or hosting a party. Her recipes are healthy enough to serve to your family, but gourmet enough to serve at a fancy gathering."

~Brianna Rossi, Mukilteo, Washington

"Thanks to Amy's suggestions for cooking larger recipes and freezing them for later, I now have delicious meals waiting in the freezer. I am not fond of cooking each day, so having main dishes handy is truly wonderful. I have acquired the necessary tools she recommended, such as the Instant Pot, the sealer, and the silicone molds."

~Barbara Culling, Venice, Florida

"I am a confirmed leftover hater. Before Amy taught me the Gourmet Done Skinny Meal Method, I relied on takeout or expensive meal-prep kits to feed my family, and dinnertime was the most stressful part of my day. I now cook healthier food that my family loves, and I am saving money. I also save time because I've learned how to food-prep the right way so the food tastes as fresh and delicious as the day I made it."

~Susan Nunley, Sacramento, California

"Food prep has always seemed like a laborious, almost unattainable, goal. Everything I read made it seem like it required hours in the kitchen. All that changed when I heard Amy speak. She gives practical suggestions, and she curates tools and appliances that have upped my game in the kitchen. I am always looking forward to her next social media post and her next tip."

~Judy Stephens, Wingo, Kentucky

"The information Amy shares in this book could make an exceptional text for one of our food studies units. Parents would love it. Teaching kids how to do meal prep at an early age . . . priceless."

~Lani Donaldson, Engaged Educators,
upacademy.ca, Calgary, Alberta, Canada

Contents

Foreword

First, let me be honest and say it's hard for me to give you a totally objective introduction to this book.

Even before I read The Power of Food Prep, I knew Amy Lawrence creates amazing resources in the world of eating and food prep, turning complicated recipes into doable ones for us non-chefs. She is a great teacher.

I'm excited for you to dive into this lovely book to learn how to make your life easier with food prep, without sacrificing taste or enjoyment.

We tend to think it takes away our pleasure when we're organized about the food we eat. We erroneously assume planning is boring and being spontaneous is where all the fun is.

Here's the truth: Some of the nicest acts of self-care you can possibly do are to plan and do some food prep for yourself. When you wait until you are so hungry you will eat anything, you ignore your needs. When you think ahead, it's like letting yourself know you are important, you are worthy, and you deserve to have yummy foods to eat when you are hungry.

That's why I advocate thinking ahead about your meals, having what you need on hand, and finally, having some of those foods ready to go.

Imagine the warm feeling you'll experience when you realize you're hungry, you open the freezer or fridge, and delicious food is waiting for you.

I know from doing this myself that it creates a warm feeling of care for myself, from myself.

Amy helps you with the nitty-gritty of getting this done in the simplest way. She gives you several choices for how to prep your food ahead of time and goes into detail, answering all the questions.

Whether you are new to food-prep or you've dabbled with it, this book provides all the tricks of the trade. Amy's here to show you how to do it in the easiest way possible. It's like having your own health-oriented private chef in your back pocket. All your questions are covered.

I have been coaching women for many years on how to stop overeating so they can lose unwanted weight. One of the key aspects of my program is to understand why our brains respond so well to thinking about what we want ahead of time. Taking actions and getting food ready ahead of time makes it easier to eat well while you eat the foods you love.

I hope you enjoy Amy's latest book as much as I have. It's a valuable how-to guide that will make your life easier, give you what you want and need when you are hungry, and add pleasure to your days.

Enjoy!
Cookie Rosenblum, Real Weight Loss for Real Women

Introduction

I've always loved cooking and planning meals. My mom's mom, Granny, was my first mentor and the strongest woman I've known. Initially a stay-at-home mom, Granny worked at a local glove factory to support her two small children after her husband suddenly passed away. They hardly had any money, and my grandmother was too proud to accept food stamps, yet I've often heard my mother say, "We didn't even know we were poor."

Granny loved to cook for her family, and you can bet there was no wasting food at her house. She saved every scrap. I still remember her bacon grease container. It was a small copper canister, and she always scraped the leftover bacon grease into it to use later. She had the tiniest kitchen, and I loved to sit on the stool and watch her make homemade noodles with her small hands. In fact, the noodle recipe in my homemade chicken noodle soup came from her. I even have a picture of her in that little kitchen. It's on my stove, and I look at her every time I cook.

Granny used to send me $3 for my birthday every year, even after I grew into adulthood. My husband would chuckle at it, but that was what she could afford. When she passed away in 2004, I was shocked to learn she left me about $10,000 in savings bonds. On top of the $3, she had purchased bonds every year for my birthday without me knowing. Those bonds added up to almost the exact amount I needed to finance one thousand copies of my first cookbook. She would have been so proud to know she financed it. Thanks to my Granny's initial investment, I've sold thousands of cookbooks over the years.

When I was nineteen, I got my first taste of catering. My dad was an officer in the Army, and when military families hosted parties, like an open house at Christmas or on New Year's Eve, the wives were expected to host, cook, and entertain, but my mom didn't like to cook. People wouldn't think about hiring a caterer in those days (not at the colonel level anyway), so my mother would call on me, and I happily stepped in to plan the menu, cook the food, and serve it. Later, when my parents were stationed in Germany and I was in college in Munich, my mom would call me to come home to help with cooking and party planning. She knew how much I loved entertaining, even then.

However much I enjoyed cooking, entertaining and restaurant management weren't on my radar as career options back then. I had wanted to be a special education teacher since second grade, so I earned degrees in education and special education and taught for eleven years before becoming a stay-at-home mom after my second child was born.

After a few years at home, I decided I needed more, but I wasn't sure what that would be. One evening, while out with my husband, I saw a tearoom. It looked so inviting, and I decided to make a reservation there the next time my mom visited. My mom and I had a delightful afternoon tea, and as we enjoyed our tea sandwiches, I noticed the gift shop had put gifts all around our table. What a unique idea! It was a lightbulb moment. I could cook and sell gifts. Soon after, I opened a tearoom in tiny Newcastle, California, near Sacramento.

I had no idea how to run a restaurant, but I made it an incredible place, a venue I would love to visit. People in town laughed at first. "Newcastle is a beer town," they said. But visitors came from all over—the Bay Area, Reno, and Lake Tahoe. We were voted Best Small Tea Room in the U.S. in 2006, Sacramento Magazine featured us a few times, and we appeared on the local TV news.

I put in a lot of hours, as did my family and especially my husband, as we managed a staff of thirteen, a restaurant, a gift shop, online sales, and inventory. My kids even helped at an early age. Thomas, my oldest son, started making tea for customers at age seven, and Jacob, who was four at the time, helped clear dishes. It was great fun for years, but a ton of hard work, and I wanted a home life again.

I closed the tearoom after six years, in 2009, and our family moved to Seattle, Washington, where I rented a commercial kitchen and sold tea online. I expanded to open a retail tea shop and blended and packed tea, selling it wholesale to other tearooms.

Tapping into my love of food in a new and different way, in 2017, I created the Gourmet Done Skinny Meal Method (although it didn't have a name at the time). It's an easy way to prep food for your family, it's not complicated, and you can apply the five simple steps to almost any recipe or diet. My method saves you time in the kitchen, preparing meals, and it works extremely well with natural eating and intuitive-eating principles.

Although I've moved a lot and experienced different careers, some things have remained constant. I still love to prep and cook meals for family and friends, I love good food, I'm fascinated by kitchen gadgets, and I'm very driven and organized. I've also experienced some personal struggles that taught me patience and flexibility and reminded me to savor every moment I can.

On my journey, I've learned my food prep ideas, which I thought were ordinary and nothing special, were eye-opening to many. Others found the way I had been cooking for years inspiring. I was thrilled and had a new calling: to inspire others to make healthy, delicious foods they could enjoy later.

In this book, I explain how, with planning and prep, you can have healthy, gourmet, home-cooked meals while cooking only a few days a week. You'll find examples of how busy women and men with little time fit these delicious meals with high-quality ingredients into their schedules. And you'll learn why you don't have to be a "Type A" person and have every meal planned out on the calendar to be successful.

So roll up your sleeves, put on your apron, grab a notebook, and get ready to learn the power of food prep.

Chapter 1:

Why Food Prep?

When I owned the tearoom, I learned how to freeze foods ahead of time and to bake and prepare them in bulk. Food, especially homemade food, can be expensive, so this was how I saved money. Food prep allowed me to cut costs and have less waste in my restaurant. We prided ourselves on making almost everything from scratch, even our croutons and salad dressings.

At the restaurant, we had Quiche Day, and I'd spend an entire day making fifty quiches at a time. Then we'd cool them and cut and freeze them as whole pies with individually cut pieces. Because we were mostly reservation only, we knew how many guests we expected each day, and the night before, we would pull out that number of quiche pieces from the freezer to thaw in the refrigerator. This was critical because we couldn't make everything homemade every day.

We mostly froze quiche, extra scones for emergencies (though we made them fresh every day), and cookie dough. We would make the cookie dough, portion it into teaspoon-size balls, using a small ice cream scoop, and then flash-freeze the balls. Again, because we knew about how many guests we'd have, we would bake the amount needed plus a few extras for the day. No waste, and our cookies were always fresh. Our customers loved our fresh, homemade food.

On busy days, we served more than one hundred people at three seatings. Sometimes I marvel at how it all worked out. I had no restaurant experience, no management experience, and no formal cooking experience. But I loved to cook and make people happy with my food, and that's what made it all work. Cooking is still my passion to this day.

I learned a lot of lessons from the restaurant that translated well to my home food prep—minus the dreaded Quiche Day, which was great when it was over, but no fun while we were in the middle of it. And that's saying something because I love to cook.

I don't like wasting food. I also want my meal plans to be flexible, so if something comes up, I can change the meal quickly. (Life with kids is crazy, and schedules often change.) But I also wanted great-tasting food, and I love having homemade food on hand in my freezer so I can whip up fantastic food creations at a moment's notice when guests unexpectedly arrive. I just needed to figure out a way to freeze it so it would stay fresh and taste freshly made when reheated.

Save Time, Money, and Calories

There are four main benefits of food prep: ease, time, money, and health/ controlled calories. Each is important in its own way.

Ease

When your food is already prepped, you can put together a meal in a hurry and you don't have to think; just combine what you have into a meal. You can use my Gourmet Done Skinny Meal Method with just about any recipe you can freeze. If you follow my steps, you won't have to cook every day. On the non-cooking days, you'll just reheat. This is great for ordinary days and extraordinary days alike.

One time my sister-in-law, Susan, and I made a long and scary drive back from Idaho through mountain passes. We didn't want to stop for food because we were afraid the pass would close because of the snow, and we were determined to get home that day. When we finally got to my house, we were tired, cold, and starving, and we didn't want to wait for pizza delivery.

I told Susan, "Let's have a bowl of my homemade chicken noodle soup. That will warm us up, and it's quick." I pulled two vacuumed-sealed portions of soup and a few pieces of homemade focaccia bread out of my freezer. I reheated the soup in the microwave for a few minutes and toasted the bread in the toaster oven, and dinner was ready. She was so impressed that we had a homemade meal in minutes that she wound up ordering a vacuum sealer when she returned home.

The ease of ready-made meals is also important when you're not feeling well or when you want to take food to others. Recently, my mother-in-law and I were talking about when she had colon cancer a few years ago. She's doing great now, but she reminded me of how I did what she considered one of the nicest things for her when she was sick. I went to her house, ordered a vacuum sealer from Amazon, same-day delivery, made her plain chicken and rice, and filled her freezer. She said it really meant a lot to her to have all those meals in her freezer when she came home from the hospital. Little did I know that the one day I decided not to visit her in the hospital, and chose instead to stay at her house to cook food for her, would make such a difference to her. That story touched my heart and is one of my favorites about food prep.

Time

If you're like most people, you think you don't have time; you think cooking is a chore, but often it's your mindset about the whole thing that stops you. Chopping vegetables can actually be relaxing. And really, how long does it take to pick up takeout or to wait for Uber Eats, DoorDash, or the pizza-delivery guy?

Lack of time is a habitual story you tell yourself. In truth, you could go to your freezer, pull out some grilled chicken, cut up some tomatoes and a few slices of onion, mash them together with an avocado, and fix yourself a Crispy Chicken Wrap—all in ten minutes. Food prep saves you time because the food is already made, and you can just pull out meals and ingredients and reheat. When you invest a little time upfront, you save hours later.

Many people don't realize the value of this method. You shop once, you cook once, you seal bags once, and you do dishes once. Contrast that with shopping multiple times in different weeks for the same meal, using three times the dishes because you prepare the recipe more than once, and cleaning three times as much. Do you like cleaning your kitchen all the time? Of course not. Why not make a bigger batch in the first place and freeze the rest for later? You'll clean up only once.

Money

You can easily save money by buying in bulk at stores like Costco and Sam's Club and cooking double or triple a recipe. Grocery stores often have deals on larger amounts as well. You'll also save money because you'll waste less with food prep. According to the USDA[1], American families spend on average about $932.20 per month on groceries for a family of four. Sadly, about forty percent of that food ends up in the trash.

With my method, because you save your leftovers in individual portions, little goes to waste. Most food-prep programs have you freeze the entire dish. Why not freeze it in portions and take out only what you need? Not only does the food thaw faster, but you save money because there's less waste.

Cooking your own food saves you a ton of money, especially when compared to takeout, DoorDash, and Uber Eats. The delivery fees are outrageous, not to mention the expensive restaurant prices and the disappointment you often feel because the food arrives cold. Meal-prep kits, like Blue Apron and others, are also incredibly expensive compared to preparing your own food.

Health/Controlled Calories

People who eat processed food eat [2] "an extra five hundred calories a day", which can equate to a two-pound weight increase per week. That's a lot of extra calories and extra weight just from eating processed food.

You'll make fewer bad choices when you've already prepared food to eat. You have the freedom to choose what you want to eat when you have something healthy in your fridge or freezer at all times—no gorging, no last-minute, order-a-pizza decisions. Not only will you eat fewer calories, but you'll also know exactly what goes into your food, and you'll

---

[1] U.S. Department of Agriculture, "The Thrifty Food Plan, 2021." Accessed July 7, 2022. fns-prod.azureedge.us/sites/default/files/media/file/CostofFoodMay2022Thrifty.pdf
[2] Kevin Hall, et al., "Ultra-Processed Diets Cause Excess Calorie Intake and Weight Gain: An Inpatient Randomized Controlled Trial of Ad Libitum Food Intake," Clinical and Translational Report. Volume 30, Issue 1, pp 67-77.E3, July 2, 2019, www.cell.com/cell-metabolism/fulltext/S1550-4131(19)30248-7 -

feel confident knowing there are no preservatives, only fresh ingredients. And the best part, it tastes better.

Think of how you feel when you eat out all the time. Lethargic? Sluggish? What happens when you cook for yourself? You feel good and you feel healthy because you're in control of what you eat. You decide what goes into your food, and you can better choices.

Everyone knows fast food isn't healthy. What you may not realize is sit-down restaurant food isn't much healthier. Restaurants add hidden calories and sodium to their entrées with fat, sugar, and processed carbs, all with the goal of enhancing the flavors and creating repeat customers. Add in extreme portion sizes, and you can imagine the added pounds just waiting to join you on the way home.

Citing studies from the University of Toronto and Tufts University that analyzed the nutritional content of food ordered at nineteen sit-down restaurant chains (not fast food), "Craving Something Healthy"[3] reports that the average meal consisted of 1,128 calories. That's fifty-six percent of the average daily 2,000-calorie intake recommended by the Food and Drug Administration for a healthy adult.

Imagine you're on vacation and eat out three times per day. That's 3,384 calories a day, an additional unneeded 1,384 calories. Even if you only eat out two meals a day, you're still adding an additional 256 calories per day if you're trying to stick to the daily 2,000-calorie limit. And that doesn't even include calories from your third meal of the day.

It's amazing how people who cook their own food have fewer health issues. My family members rarely get a cold, and I swear it's because we eat fresh food and not all the junk. When you make good choices in what you prepare, homemade food is just better for you.

---

[3] Anne Danahy, "The Real (Calorie) Cost of Dining Out," accessed July 7, 2022, cravingsomethinghealthy.com/the-real-calorie-cost-of-dining-out/

Food prep reduces stress, which is a big deal for health maintenance. When you're stressed and hungry, and trying to put together healthy meals amid a busy schedule, you're more likely to make poor choices. It's not that I never order pizza. I do, but I order it because I choose to, not because I'm stressed about time. Once you get into the habit of food prep, you'll always have a ton of healthy choices available in your freezer, and you can eat out or order in when you prefer to, not because you're too stressed to cook.

The Full Picture

Here's a real-life example that puts this all together, so you can see the full picture of benefits. Think how much money you could save if you meal-prepped my Chipotle Egg Cups even once a month. My friend Lola buys Starbucks egg bites a few times a week. According to her, they cost $4.35 for two. Her usual breakfast order is $12.15, which includes a large tea, egg bites, and banana bread.

The Bacon and Gruyere Egg Bites are 300 calories for two, while the Egg Whites and Red Pepper Bites are 180 calories. My Chipotle Egg Cups are bigger (you can eat just one) and are 101 calories per cup. Not only are they made with fresh ingredients, but you can also make twenty-four egg cups in an hour and have twenty-four breakfasts ready to go in the freezer. You can heat them in the microwave in about one minute and fifteen seconds, and they cost about forty-eight cents per cup.

If Lola eats at Starbucks three times a week, ordering two egg bites and a cup of tea each time, that's $8.60 per day, or $103.20 per month, just on breakfast. If she eats two egg cups at home and makes her own tea three times per week, that's only $11.52 per month. Homemade is healthier and a lot cheaper. And you save gas and time by eating at home. Even better!

Making your own gourmet meals and doing your own food prep not only saves money, calories, and time, but it's also so much healthier. You feel better when you eat better, and that's the best reason of all to meal-prep. Eating out is a habit. Food-prepping is a habit. Change your habit.

How Is This Method Different from Other Meal-Prep Methods?

The Gourmet Done Skinny Meal Method focuses on quality food. It's about taste and preservation. Some recipes do take some time to make because they include fresh ingredients and fresh herbs, but you don't have to do a bunch of cooking in one day, which can leave you exhausted and never wanting to cook again.

Instead, Gourmet Done Skinny allows you to make beautiful meals three days a week, freeze the extras, and enjoy them on another day. My recipes use real food ingredients, like garlic, rosemary, and butter. Some of this takes time to prepare, like peeling the garlic or chopping the rosemary, but those fresh ingredients matter.

Some of my recipes use my "special" ingredients, which are often other homemade recipes I've previously frozen. It makes such a difference when you use my Parmesan Chicken Broth instead of store-bought chicken broth. Although you can certainly substitute store-bought broth, the taste isn't as good. The fresh ingredients I use make a huge difference. But do I want to make Parmesan Chicken Broth every time I need it? No, that's why I figured out a way to preserve it, so I can have it at the ready in one-cup and half-cup portions. (For my Parmesan Chicken Broth, visit

Gourmetdoneskinny.com/recipes/freezer-friendly/easy-instant-pot-parmesan-broth)

With my method, all the foods you freeze will taste as delicious as the day you cooked them. I'm a foodie. I take recipes to the next level because I go the extra mile with my ingredients. What you put into it determines what you get out of it.

Granted, not everyone goes to such lengths or cares as much about the quality of their food. And while I thoroughly enjoy cooking, I don't want to spend two hours on a meal every day. It's all about balance—having great, healthy, gourmet food and balance in life.

How Does This Method Compare to Programs Like HelloFresh, Blue Apron, and Others?

While meal-prep services like these are a great help to some people, they also serve a slightly different purpose than my Gourmet Done Skinny Meal Method. Their goal is to give you exact proportions so there are no leftovers, which means you still have to cook every day.

Cooking and food-prepping your own food may seem like a lot of work compared to meal services that bring the recipe and groceries to you. However, you benefit a lot more when you do it yourself. Not only do you get to pick exactly what foods you want to eat, but you also know where your food comes from and exactly what is in your meal. You save a lot of money and calories, and you have leftovers for another time. Consider some pros and cons below.

Gourmet Done Skinny Meal Method - Pros
- Save money.
- Make your favorite foods.
- Eat your favorite foods more often.
- Know what goes into your food.

- Control your portion sizes.
- Cut calories.
- Don't cook every day.

Gourmet Done Skinny Meal Method - Cons

- Shop for or order the right amount of groceries for recipes.
- Decide what you're making, instead of choosing from a small list.

Prepared-Food Companies (Like HelloFresh, Blue Apron, Home Chef) - Pros

- Meals come to you ready to cook with no need to shop.
- You choose from a small list, preventing overwhelm.
- Meals are portioned, which can be good and bad.

Prepared-Food Companies (Like HelloFresh, Blue Apron, Home Chef) - Cons

- There are no extras if someone stops by for dinner at the last minute.
- You can't freeze extras for later.
- You're limited to their list and can't order your favorite meals again and again.
- Meals are more expensive.
- Special dietary needs and picky eaters aren't typically considered with meal options.
- The calorie count is much higher, and the food is sometimes less nutritious. (One company has meals at 900 calories or more per serving. That's a lot!)

The biggest disadvantage with ordering delivery meals is that you still have to cook every night. With the Gourmet Done Skinny Meal Method, you cook three times per week and pull items from your freezer the rest of the week. Because everything is vacuum sealed, your meals always taste fresh. They are planned extras, not the dreaded leftovers most people think of when they think of cooking extra food.

Gourmet Food Prep Q&A

I grew up eating leftovers and hated them as a child. We seemed to have the same meal three days in a row. How is your method different?

I'm with you. If you grew up eating leftovers, you might have an aversion to them for a few reasons. Maybe the ingredients weren't super fresh, or maybe your mom used more canned goods and spices instead of fresh produce and herbs. It could be you simply got tired of the food because you had to eat it three days in a row, rather than freezing it to enjoy another time. Or perhaps the leftovers were reheated incorrectly.

With the Gourmet Done Skinny Meal Method, all the recipes start with delicious, fresh, flavorful ingredients. You don't get tired of them because you only eat a meal on one day, and you freeze the rest to enjoy another time. I've also developed the best ways to reheat my recipes so they taste as delicious out of the freezer as the day you made them.

CHAPTER 2:

Be a Foodie and Eat Healthy

In 2014, my retail tea shop and commercial kitchen was running beautifully in a charming area called Country Village, in Bothell, Washington. I was finally making good money and life was great. Then a friend visited from Sacramento, and I showed her my Pilates Reformer exercise equipment and one of my favorite Pilates moves. The next morning, I had a horrible headache and neck ache. I went to the emergency room, but they didn't know what the cause was, so they sent me home.

The next day, my headache was much worse, so I went back to the emergency room. They said it was just a tension headache, which I knew in my heart was wrong. Sometimes you really should trust your gut, but I didn't do that. Instead, I went with their advice. They told me to do an exercise where I'd tilt my head to one side and pull my head down with my hands. When I did that, I felt something pop.

Instantly, the room started spinning. But because I had been to the ER twice, and they didn't seem to think the issue was anything serious, I went to bed. At two in the morning, my son texted me to let me know he had made a flight. My head pain was excruciating, so I decided to take another pain pill but realized I couldn't swallow, so I woke up my husband. Although I was slurring my speech and couldn't walk very well, I thought I was normal, but my husband knew something was majorly wrong. We raced to the hospital.

It turned out I had experienced a mild stroke from a vertebral artery dissection, a slow leak in an artery in my neck caused from a tear doing the Pilates move a few days earlier. When I performed the tension headache exercise, I tore it further. I spent a week in the ICU and another week in the hospital. I was lucky to be alive.

I couldn't do anything in the beginning, which was frightening. I lay there, wondering whether I would ever get out of that hospital bed and whether my husband would have to take care of me forever.

I started physical therapy while in the hospital and began walking again. As I slowly reemerged into my life, I realized I didn't want to go back to running the business I had created. My manager, Brianna, had taken over for nearly six months during my recovery, but she wanted to start a family. I thought, *I don't want to train anybody else. I think I'm done.* I called one of my wholesale tea customers, told him I was selling my business, and asked if he wanted to buy it. He did.

When my husband came home that night, I said, "Well, I sold the business."

"You did what?" he asked. He was shocked, but I knew it was the right thing to do.

I felt lucky to be alive, so I celebrated life in the simplest way I knew how. I ate. I thought, *I'm eating whatever the heck I want.* I wanted to enjoy life, and I did.

After making the decision to close my business in 2016, I decided to visit India on a tea tour. When I returned, I looked at the pictures taken of me while I was there. *Oh my god, I look so bad*, I thought. I had gained forty pounds, eating whatever I wanted after the stroke. I was never an emotional eater, but at that time, happy to be alive, I celebrated with food. I ate the hamburgers, the fries, everything.

To eliminate the added pounds, I joined a weight loss program in 2017, but I was dissatisfied with their recipes. They were bland and tasteless, so I started to create my own recipes and entered them in their recipe calculator to figure out the points. I had already written ten cookbooks with my tea business, but those were recipes full of fat, butter, and sugar, so they weren't what I needed on this leg of my journey. This time, I lightened up old favorites and created healthy new ones.

I had so much fun creating and eating these new healthy recipes that I thought others might enjoy them too. Thus, my blog, *Gourmet Done Skinny*, was born.

While following the weight loss plan and using my own recipes, I lost about forty pounds, and I also created a new career. My objective was to help others eat healthy and enjoy gourmet food without restrictive meal plans that didn't offer flavor or flexibility.

At the end of 2020, I joined Cookie Rosenblum's Weight Loss Made Real program and started listening to my body and its needs. Although I had lost a lot of weight with the other program, I was bored and frustrated with the restrictive diets. I was tired of saving my points for the weekend, tired of thinking about food and my next meal all the time, and tired of the whole weight loss game. I had given food all the power. As Cookie says, "I wanted to lose the *whole* problem."

Earlier that year, I had experienced another huge blow with a flare-up of my rheumatoid arthritis. Mine isn't caused by diet, but is triggered by stress. I could barely use my hands or walk, and I had to wait nearly eight months for doctors to find the right meds. That time was absolute hell, but looking back, I realized it taught me patience and appreciation for what my body could do.

I learned to live each moment and be more grateful. Now, I write in my gratitude journal every day, jotting down even the smallest things I'm grateful for, like holding a cup of tea. Life is too short to take anything for granted. This time in my life taught me the truth behind the concept of "Do what you love, and the rest will follow."

Intuitive Eating and Being a Natural Eater

You may have heard the term "intuitive eating" without knowing what it meant. The concept has been around for quite a while and is not a diet but more like an anti-diet. It's a different way of eating, in which foods are not considered "good" or "bad." Basically, you listen to your body and eat what feels right for you. Sound simple? It is, and it isn't. Once you get the principles down, then it is fairly easy. But it can take a lot of emotional work to get there.

The Gourmet Done Skinny Meal Method works extremely well with natural eating and intuitive-eating principles. You consider what your body is hungry for, go to your freezer or fridge, pull out what sounds good to eat, and eat just enough to satisfy your hunger. It's as simple as that.

When you listen to your body and eat good, healthy food, you strengthen your immune system, curb your cravings, and gain energy. What you put into your body really does matter. When you cut down on the processed food, you'll be amazed at how much better you feel.

There are a few principles to follow with natural eating. **First, eat only when you're slightly hungry.** Not starved, not hangry, not when others are eating, not because it's lunchtime, but when you feel it's time to eat.

For some, a sign of hunger can be a rumbling of the stomach. For others, it can be a light-headedness. Hunger signals can be different for everyone, but they come from true hunger, not because "Oh, that cookie sounds good."

Second, stop eating when you're slightly full. This can also mean different things to different people, but you don't eat until you feel stuffed. You discover over time and with practice what amount fills you up. Take time to savor the experience and the food. Focus on every bite and stop when you're satisfied. When I eat out, I think, *You can waste it on your waist, or you can waste it in the trash.* Eat what you want and throw away the rest, or save it for later if possible.

Third, quit using food as a comfort or your only source of self-care. Choose foods that make you feel good, and eating a bunch of sugar doesn't make your body feel good. Filling it with nutritious foods makes your body feel good and run efficiently. I choose nutritious foods about eighty percent of the time, but I do allow myself treats. I eat cookies, hamburgers, and fries, and I drink wine, but those treats are not what my body craves. It craves avocados, meat and yogurt, to name a few foods. Moderation in enjoying treats is the key. You already know what foods are good for you; you don't have to be told.

Fourth, emotions and thoughts play a huge role in intuitive eating. Ask yourself, "Am I truly physically hungry? Would a banana take this hunger away?" Much of the time when you think you're physically hungry, you are hungry for other things, like self-care. That was my problem. My chosen form of self-care was eating, rather than doing other things to honor myself. Food might seem to solve your problems temporarily, but it really doesn't. When you turn to food to do anything other than nourish your body, you are not responding to true physical hunger. You're pacifying yourself and possibly avoiding the real issue. Your thoughts control your feelings and actions. It's up to you to change your thoughts.

Although all these principles sound easy, they're not until you really delve in and figure out why you're eating more than you should. I learned many of these principles and more from Cookie Rosenblum in her Freedom Group Program. You can find her program at: realweightlossrealwomen.com.

When you quit feeding your body yucky crap, many of those bad cravings go away. Food companies put in addictive additives to make you crave their food. Processed food is loaded with salt, which makes you want more. After you've had enough salt, you have a craving for sugar. You seesaw back and forth between wanting sugar and wanting salt.

Real food—fresh vegetables and whole fruit—takes those cravings away. To learn more about what food companies are doing with our food, check out *The End of Overeating: Taking Control of the Insatiable American Appetite*, by David A. Kessler, MD. It's a fascinating read from a former Food and Drug Administration commissioner about the food industry's aggressive marketing tactics and how they are making us sick.

It's sad that food companies add things to foods so consumers crave them and, in a sense, become "addicted" and buy more. No wonder so many Americans are overweight. And the sad thing is that the younger generation is growing up on all this bad food, so they often have no clue how to listen to their body's real needs.

When you listen to your body and gut, you feel better. Ask yourself before you sit down with friends and family, "Am I really hungry?" If you're not, don't eat. This can be hard to do, especially when you're around others who are eating, but pay attention to your body's signals. Most likely, whenever you've overeaten or eaten poorly your body craves something healthy for the next meal. Why? Because your body is craving vegetables, something lighter, something healthier that includes the nutrients it didn't get in the previous meal.

You know when you've gone overboard, and you pay for it by being mentally and physically lethargic. Think about how you feel after the holidays: so fat, stuffed, and uncomfortable that you can't wait to start a new diet in January. Your body knows when you've had enough. The problem is you don't always listen to your body before it's too late. You need to start paying attention now.

As a natural eater, I'm now in the habit of eating Cookie's way. I rarely overeat anymore. I eat until my body is satisfied and no more. If I don't finish a portion, I put it in the fridge for later. This contrasts with my childhood when we neither wasted food nor saved it for later. We ate what was on our plate at that meal. "There are starving kids in Africa," my parents said back then.

The beauty of my Gourmet Done Skinny Meal Method is that you thaw only the portion you think you might eat. If you don't finish it, you can always save it for a later time, but the food doesn't go to waste.

Chapter 3

The Gourmet Done Skinny
Meal Method in 5 Simple Steps

Imagine you've just returned home from a long trip. Everyone is cranky, starving, tired of eating out, and tired of spending money. And of course they are looking to you for food.

You go to your freezer and magically pull out four individual meatloaves you made three months earlier and a few slices of that delicious cheese bread from Costco. You might not have any fresh vegetables in the refrigerator because you were gone for a week and the fridge is bare, but no one cares. You microwave the meatloaf, toast the bread, and your quick dinner is done. All in a matter of minutes. Everyone is happy. No waiting for delivery from Uber Eats or DoorDash, no expensive takeout. It's good food, and it's fast and easy.

On another day, you're feeling a little creative in the kitchen but don't want to start from scratch. You go to your freezer, pull out some Spicy Vegetarian Meatballs (See recipe on p. 163.) and a packet of Homemade Tomato Sauce (See recipe on p. 127.). You chop some fresh onions, zucchini and red peppers, and sauté the onions for a few minutes. Finally you add the other veggies and the vegetarian meatballs. While the veggies are cooking, you boil some water for pasta. Then you toss it all together for an easy meal in less than thirty minutes. All homemade, all delicious, no preservatives, and all great for you.

Do these examples sound glorious? Are you wondering how you prepare all this fabulous food so you can reap the benefits of your efforts on days when you don't have a creative bone in your body or the energy to make a big meal? It's easy, and I'll show you how.

The Gourmet Done Skinny Meal Method includes just five simple steps to plan, prepare, and store meals:

1. Pick three meals to make for the week, and choose your prep option. (Use the recipes in the back of this book, check out my website, or use your own recipes).
2. Plan the grocery list and get the ingredients.
3. Cook.
4. Portion.
5. Vacuum seal and freeze.

Steps 4 and 5 are the two essential secrets critical to the Gourmet Done Skinny Meal Method and distinguish it from other prep methods. I'll explain in more detail below.

You'll need a handful of kitchen tools to get started. You can add gadgets as you go, but some important ones to have on hand from the beginning include a vacuum sealer, a good chopping knife, and an Instant Pot.

One of your key decisions is to choose your prep option before you start. This is your food-prep strategy and is a personal choice, depending on your available time, energy, and preferred style. You might decide to make everything in one day, to prep a certain type of food, or to double up on batches as you go.

I'll explain all the options in detail, but if you need to fill your freezer fast, you might choose prep option C, Big Cook Day. If you don't have much time, you might choose prep option A, Multiply It, and if you have picky or special eaters, you might choose prep option B, Batch It. You can use one or all of them, depending on what you're making and the time you have.

Most of the time, I use Multiply It and double or triple a recipe and then freeze the extras. I use Batch It for special meals and do a Big Cook Day occasionally or when I know I have a lot of company visiting.

Food Prep Options

Prep Option A – Multiply It: Double or triple the recipe every time you cook.

This is my favorite way to food-prep and what I consider the easiest way. It does take some time to build up a supply of various foods in your freezer with Multiply It, but this option barely affects your day-to-day routine.

Pick three days of the week to cook. On the other days, you can eat the leftovers, pull something out of the freezer, or have a night out. If you need to change your cook night, it won't matter after you've been doing this for a while.

Whenever you make dinner, double or triple the recipe. Seriously, it's that simple. It saves cooking time, dishwashing time, and prep time because you only cook, prep, and wash dishes once. Of course, if you picked a big recipe that takes a lot of prep, you might save that for prep option C, Big Cook Day. But for a simple thirty-minute recipe, it's usually easy to double or triple it without much extra work.

Think about it. If I told you to make Instant-Pot Korean Beef (See recipe on p. 115.) three separate times, how long would that take you? It's an easy and fast dish, but when you make the dish three different times, it takes so much more effort. You have to shop and gather the ingredients three times, cut and sauté the onions three times, brown the beef three times, measure the other ingredients three times, and wait for the meal to cook three times. Then you also have to wash and put away the dishes three times. So why not double or triple the recipe in the first place and then freeze the extras every time you cook?

Once you get into the routine of making extras every time you cook, it becomes a habit. Eventually you'll have a nice selection of frozen meals to choose from in your freezer.

Prep Option B – Batch It: Make just one item or meal, and freeze.

This option works well if you want to make a batch of something to freeze right away—like Chipotle Egg Cups (See recipe on p. 107.), individual meatloaves, or a bunch of grilled chicken. You make one batch; then pack it and freeze it.

For the chicken, I buy a big pack (about seven pounds) of boneless, skinless thighs at Costco. I brine them overnight and grill them with my Homemade Chipotle Seasoning (See recipe on p. 105.) the next day. When finished, I chop them into bite-size pieces, package into one-cup portions, and freeze. If I don't have time to do all the prep at once, I'll grill the chicken and pack and seal on another day. When I need chicken for tacos, pizza, salad, or pasta, I just pull out the number of packs I need.

Batch It is also a great option if you're making a special meal for someone. When I make my vegan enchiladas for my mom, before she comes to visit, I make one batch and freeze the enchiladas in individual portions. When everyone is visiting and we have chicken enchiladas, I'll pull out a vegan enchilada for her.

Does your family have fussy eaters? A great solution for families with various food preferences (like the teenage daughter who decided to go vegan last month) is to keep foods they like on hand in your freezer. This option is also good if you're only cooking for one or two people. Most recipes make four servings, so cooking one full recipe and freezing the rest makes sense for a smaller household.

Prep Option C – Big Cook Day: Plan a big cook day and make a ton.

This option is what most people think of when they think of meal prep, and it stresses them out because they think they must dedicate one whole weekend day a few times a month. If you incorporate my other options in your food prep, you never have to do that. But of course, you can choose this option if you want to. And it's also a great way to stock your freezer quickly.

There are a few times when I feel the bigger cook day is necessary, like special occasions or more work-intensive dishes. For example, I always do it when I make my chicken enchiladas. They're a lot of work, so it makes sense to make a lot and schedule the whole day for prep. I also choose Big Cook Day for my Healthier Apple Dumplings. (You can find this recipe at Gourmetdoneskinny.com/recipes/dessert/healthier-homemade-apple-dumplings) It's kind of a big deal to core all the apples, make the pastry, roll it out, and put the dumplings together. It also takes a lot of work to make homemade lasagna, so when I do it, I want to make it count. I use the day to make a lot of lasagna.

When you choose Big Cook Day, make it fun, and try to include the entire family. You can even invite your neighbors and friends for a big cooking party.

The 5 Steps of the Gourmet Done Skinny Meal Method

Step 1: Pick three meals.

Choose three different meals for the week, and decide on your prep option (Multiply It, Batch It, or Big Cook Day). Go to the end of this book or check out my food blog, gourmetdoneskinny.com, for recipes. If you know you don't have much time that week, choose meals that are fast and easy to prepare, and choose prep option A, Multiply It. I try to be consistent about the day I plan my meals and shop. You'll read more about this in the Sunday Plan-and-Clean-Out Day.

Step 2: Plan the grocery list.

See what you have, first, and then make a list of what you need. Go to Costco or the grocery store, or order your groceries. If you're doubling recipes, don't forget to account for that on your grocery list. Add in fresh vegetables and fruits for side dishes.

Side dishes don't have to be elaborate—roasted veggies, steamed cauliflower, broccoli, or carrots will do. Just try to incorporate them into your everyday meals. The weight problem in the U.S. exists partly because we often skip the veggies when they should make up a huge portion of our meal. Ideally, we should have a small amount of the main dish and a larger amount of fruits and vegetables, so don't forget to include them on your shopping list.

Buy in bulk. Depending on your list, buying in bulk can make a lot of sense. It's often less expensive to grill and pack chicken when you buy a big package from stores like Costco and Sam's Club. I often buy large packages of ground turkey and hamburger and divide them into smaller two-pound packages to use later. Buying in bulk can save you a lot of money.

Divide the shopping and cooking tasks. If you hate to shop, maybe have your spouse do all the shopping, and then you do the cooking.

Shop online. Many people think online shopping is too expensive, but consider how valuable your time is to you. If you dread going grocery shopping, ordering online is a great option. You can even tell Alexa to add items to your shopping list so you don't have to spend time writing them down. Shopping online makes your life easier, helps you spend less by not overbuying, and is more convenient because everything arrives at your door.

Even with grocery pickup, you get many of these benefits. How many times have you made an impulse buy in the store because "Oh, that sounds good!"? When you shop online, you buy exactly what's on your list and no more. Think of all the items you bring home after a grocery store trip that weren't on the list. Besides, online shopping may not be as expensive as you think. Most stores will even waive the delivery fee if you buy over a certain amount.

Another benefit of shopping online is that the apps often show you what you bought last or frequently purchased items. This is handy and helps you remember items you might have forgotten. Plus, ordering groceries online is quick. With a few keystrokes, your list is done, and groceries are on their way to you. While I love to cook, I really don't like to grocery shop, thus my love of online grocery shopping. I often do a combination of Costco and online shopping, so I don't have to go to the grocery store.

Choose the best ingredients. Choose fresh ingredients when you're cooking. Not only will they taste better, but they'll also keep in the freezer better. Great places to find fresh ingredients include local farmer's markets, fruit and vegetable stands, and grocery stores with high-end produce. What you put into your dish makes a difference. Make every bite count.

Also, I recommend growing your own herbs and vegetables if possible. I love to make lots of pesto with my fresh basil in the summer. I freeze it in small cubes. In winter, when fresh basil is nonexistent in the grocery store, I'll just add a little of my frozen pesto to a dish where I need some fresh-basil taste.

Step 3: Cook.

Make cooking fun. Start by making sure you have time to enjoy it. Then enlist family members to help. Put on music or a favorite TV show; open a bottle of wine and have a glass while you're rocking out to the music and chopping vegetables. Many people think of cooking as a chore, but if you change your mindset, it can be a really good experience, alone or with family or friends.

Step 4: Portion.

After you prepare your meal and eat it for dinner, the food prep magic begins. Pull out a measuring cup and scoop portions into bags, vacuum seal them, and freeze. Or if you know you're going to eat the food in a few days, put it in a container and label it. I like to use the black prep boxes for short-term food storage. Too tired after dinner? No worries. Ask the kids or your roommate to do it, or save the portioning for another day and put the food in the refrigerator. Just be sure to bag and vacuum seal it all by the fourth day after cooking.

Portions are the key to your food prep. When you need a quick lunch or dinner, you can go to your freezer and pull out exactly what you need. No thawing out big containers of soup or casserole that go to waste. You pull out exactly the number of portions you need.

Have extra artisan bread that you bought at Costco? Freeze two or three slices in a pack. The next time you have soup, toast those pieces to go along with your meal. Nothing gets wasted.

How many times have you frozen a huge chunk of something? It takes forever to thaw, even in the microwave. And you still end up throwing away whatever you don't eat. Why not save food in the first place and portion it all out, so later you can take out exactly what you need? If you need more, it's easy to grab another package and thaw it out quickly. Many people don't even think about portioning out casseroles or lasagna, but having single servings of these dishes in the freezer is so valuable.

Portion grilled chicken in one-cup portions and store using a vacuum sealer.

Step 5: Vacuum seal and freeze.

Vacuum sealing and freezing are critical parts of my method that so many other food-prep programs do not include. When you use a vacuum sealer, it deprives your food of oxygen, and without oxygen, mold and bacteria cannot grow. Vacuum sealing also protects food from freezer burn, which occurs when food loses moisture. Freezer burn makes the food dry and tough, and I've found it can happen even with those products marketed specifically for freezer storage.

To preserve quality meals and retain their fresh taste, you must use a vacuum sealer to protect your meals. Meals frozen in the vacuum-sealed bags last three to five times longer than food stored in containers or plastic bags. Vacuum-sealed meals kept in the freezer can last one to two years and still taste fantastic. Foods frozen in regular plastic bags get freezer burned very quickly. Think about how much less you would have to cook if you could effectively store your meals in the freezer for longer periods of time.

Think about how valuable it would be to pull food out of your freezer that will actually taste good when it's reheated. That's the whole point of my method. You want the food to taste as good as the day you cooked it. And when you use my Gourmet Done Skinny Meal Method, it will.

That's it. That's my method. Keep reading to see how it all works together.

Should you do food prep if you have only one or two people living at home?

Yes, of course. Food prep is perfect for any size household. If you have a small household, like one to two people, choose prep option B, Batch It. Make a meal that serves four, then freeze the leftovers in individual portions.

When you want soup or casserole, just take out the number of portions you need. In your case, you probably don't need to cook three times a week. So maybe two times will work for you. You still have to eat, but you don't have to cook every day. Consider giving extra food to neighbors or entertaining friends.

Isn't it nice to just go to the freezer and pull something out for dinner? Normally people freeze casseroles, lasagnas, or soups in one big portion, but if you do it in individual portions, you'll always have something easy and quick to eat.

Chapter 4:

Putting It All Together

I recently inspired my sister-in-law to start doing food prep. She's amazed at how much less stress she feels, knowing she has a plan and food in the freezer. She's a realtor with an extremely busy job, and she and her husband have four kids, ages seventeen to thirty, two of whom live at home. Everyone is on different schedules and looks to her every day to ask what's for dinner. Planning nightly dinners was taking a lot of her mental energy. After I explained she only had to pick three meals, cook three times a week, and then freeze the leftovers, she was excited.

My sister-in-law had used HelloFresh for a while and loved having meals delivered to her door, but she became dissatisfied because she felt they were expensive. She also disliked that she couldn't keep reordering her favorite meals, only what was offered each week. The meals were also higher in calories, and there weren't any leftovers. If her two daughters stopped by, there wasn't enough food, or she had to supplement the meals with extra chicken, beef, or some other meat. Most of all, she didn't like that she had to cook every night of the week because there were no leftovers.

Using the Gourmet Done Skinny Meal Method, she now cooks less, which has lowered her stress level. She's even included her oldest son in the food-prep process. He helped her figure out how to use her new vacuum sealer, and they enjoy cooking and prepping together.

Here's a quick review of the process:
1. Choose three meals for the week and a prep option.
2. Make a grocery list, and shop for the food.
3. Cook on three days.
4. Put this week's leftovers in the fridge.
5. Portion, vacuum seal, and freeze the extras.

Helpful Definitions

Food-Prep/Ingredient-Prep: Make sure all the parts are ready before you cook. When most people think of food prep, they think about making the entire meal. Few people think about the parts, like having grilled chicken in your freezer and ready to go, which you could use in a variety of meals.

Food prep can mean chopping the vegetables or making sure the sauces and broths are already made and stored in the freezer. It could also mean lettuce is in the refrigerator, already washed, or carrots are cut and ready for snacking. The parts are prepped.

Meal-Prep: This involves putting the meal together—assembling the parts, getting a casserole, lasagna, or main dish ready to go in the oven or in the freezer.

Ask yourself what items you need to begin this process and what the parts are. If I'm making lasagna, I need to have the noodles cooked, the meat mixture made, and the cheese shredded. Meal-prepping means making the lasagna and putting it together. If I'm making a casserole, this might mean combining the already cooked rice with the cooked chicken and then mixing in the sauce and baking it all in the oven.

Meal Planning and "What's for dinner tonight?": This is putting all components of a meal together, deciding what you're having for the main dish, side dishes, and dessert. Meal planning is pulling the lasagna pieces out of the freezer, making a salad, and figuring out if you want a bit of dessert to go with it. But with my method, you don't have to have your meals all planned out on the calendar. You can decide what you're in the mood for on the fly.

After you have picked out your three meals to make for the week, meal planning becomes very easy. Choose what you're having either in the morning or when you get home from work. Choose to cook that night or pull something out of the freezer (that you have cooked previously). Because you've planned your three meals for the week, you have all the ingredients you need, and you have options.

After you have chosen the main part of the meal, decide whether you'll have the roasted veggies for a side dish or some steamed broccoli. I find sides are fairly easy for most people. They don't have to be elaborate. Steamed broccoli, side salad, even a quick tomato salad with fresh basil, and a little salt and pepper works great as a side dish. Try to incorporate as many vegetables as you can.

Although it's tempting to make just the main dish, don't skip the side dish. That's one thing our society is lacking these days. We concentrate so much on the main dish that we skip the sides, when in reality, we should be eating more vegetables and fruit and only a small portion of the main dish. The big calories usually come from the main dish, not the sides. Vegetables fill you up, and you will eat less of the main dish. That's another way to save some calories.

On days when you're not cooking or not cooking as much, just go to your freezer and mix and match what you want to eat. What sounds good for dinner tonight? Grilled chicken, homemade tomato sauce, and pasta? Meatloaf? Enchiladas? With some roasted cauliflower or roasted veggies? It's that simple. Be patient, though. It does take a bit of time, at first, to stock your freezer, but after you make the Gourmet Done Skinny Meal Method a habit, you'll have a lot of options to choose from.

Just this morning my mom told me on the phone, "Your dad was so thrilled with dinner last night. When I reorganized my freezer this week, I found your frozen homemade barbecue sauce. I took out the barbecue sauce and some leftover steak you had frozen for us from Christmas when you were here, and I put it all together. He was so happy." (On a side note, my mom is vegan and my dad isn't, so he's thrilled anytime he can get steak.)

In Action: From Grocery List to Grocery Store to Preparing the Meals

On Sunday, I choose the three meals I want to make for the week and which prep option I'm using for those meals. I mostly choose prep option A, Multiply It, because that works best with my schedule, and I will usually ask my family which meals they want or just make their favorites. I check my pantry, freezer, and fridge to decide what ingredients I need to make the dishes. Many of my recipes have ingredients I already have on hand such as onions or potatoes.

Next, I write out my grocery list. I add lots of fresh vegetables and herbs because I like to use veggies for side dishes. I also add a few pieces of fruit.

Then, I pick a day to go to both Costco and the grocery store (or I order the veggies from Amazon Fresh and just go to Costco). My best advice: never plan on cooking the same day you go grocery shopping. It sounds great at the time. While you're in the store, you make all these grand plans for dinner, but once you actually get home and unload the groceries, you're just too tired to make a meal. So plan on pulling something out of the freezer for dinner that night. Trust me, you'll thank me later.

Last, I cook on my cook day(s). If something happens during the day and I can't cook, I just pull something out of the freezer. Because everything is in individual portions, it doesn't take long to reheat. If you like everything planned out, you could write what meal you are making on the calendar. I don't. I just go to my fridge that day, see what sounds good from my three choices and what I have time for, and cook. Because I have the ingredients already purchased and in the fridge, it's pretty easy to decide.

Sunday Plan-and-Clean-Out Day

One of the best things you can do for yourself is be consistent with your planning. A little effort each week goes a long way and saves you a ton of time later. I'll use Sunday for my example because it's what works well with my schedule, but you choose a day that works best for your schedule.

Every Sunday, look in your refrigerator and see what you have. Do you have any vegetables that need to be eaten right away? If so, you might make my Spicy Roasted Vegetables (See recipe on p. 155.). Or maybe this is a good day to make Refrigerator Stir Fry (See recipe on p. 159.) from those vegetables. Or you can freeze those carrots and other vegetables to make bone broth or soup later.

Do you have any fruit that needs to be eaten? If so, think about juicing it and freezing it for later.

This is also the day to see what you need for the week based on what you already have. Look at the dates on those black prep boxes. Is the food still okay to eat? If not, it's time to get rid of it. Hopefully your family has been paying attention all week and there aren't too many leftovers in the refrigerator. If it's food you have previously frozen and pulled out for meals, and it's not eaten in a day or two, it's time to throw it out. If you just made the meal this week, and you're on day four or less, then package and freeze it if it's a freezable meal. Just remember never to re-freeze something you already pulled out of the freezer. Freeze one time only for safety reasons.

If you are faithful about the Sunday plan-and-clean-out day, your life will be so much easier. Starting Monday with a plan and a clean fridge is such a great feeling. Trust me on this.

Side Dishes and Vegetables

In addition to making the three meals a week, I typically make my Spicy Roasted Veggies (See recipe on p. 155.) or my Roasted Indian Cauliflower Vegetable Medley (See recipe on p. 157.). Roasted veggies are my secret way to stay trim and are part of my weekly meal plan. I learned a few years ago that the best way for me to stay full and satisfied is to eat lots of vegetables for snacks as well as meals. Unfortunately, raw vegetables are sometimes too hard on my digestive system, but roasted vegetables are fine and taste great.

A nonstick roasting pan is key when you are roasting vegetables. With a nonstick pan, you don't have to use a lot of oil and the vegetables don't stick to the pan. I use my nonstick roasting pan all the time. Every Sunday I make a big pan of roasted vegetables. Often, these are the vegetables that need to be eaten right away before they go bad. After roasting, I put them in a few containers and use them throughout the week. It makes my life so easy having them already roasted. I just grab and go.

How do I incorporate roasted vegetables into my day?

- **Put them in a breakfast burrito.** If I'm not eating my Chipotle Egg Cups (See recipe on p. 107.) or Skillet Scramble, (recipe on my website) I throw the vegetables into my breakfast burrito—a medley of eggs, bacon bits, and a bit of cheese—and wrap them in one of my homemade tortillas (premade, stored in the freezer).

- **Eat them as snacks.** Often around 10:30 a.m., I'm hungry, so I heat up a bowl of roasted veggies and they keep me full until lunch.

- **Put them over salad greens.** Add some grilled chicken and a bit of my Healthy Garlic Ranch and Dip, Healthy Creamy Parmesan Herb Dressing and Dip, or my favorite, Skinny Blue Cheese Dressing and Dip. (See recipes on my website, and on p. 153). This lunch will keep you full until dinner time. You can warm the vegetables or leave them cold.

- **Put them in wraps.** Add a bit of grilled chicken for a great filling lunch.

- **Use them as a side dish for dinner.** Make your main dish and reheat the roasted vegetables for a complete meal.

Best Vegetables for Roasting

Use whatever veggies you like most. I just throw whatever I have into my roasting pan on Sunday, but it all depends on what you like.

Here are some of my favorites and regulars:

- mushrooms (If my family is eating the veggies, then I must roast the mushrooms separately, as no one else in my family likes them.)
- red, yellow, and green peppers
- onions (Make sure you don't mince them. Use bigger chunks. Otherwise it steams the veggies, and they become mushy.)
- fresh green beans
- zucchini (Use bigger chunks so they don't become mushy.)
- butternut squash
- asparagus
- jalapeño
- garlic
- potatoes (Use only one or two.)
- sweet potatoes (Use only one or two.)
- broccoli
- cauliflower (I have a special recipe for roasted cauliflower that I often alternate with the Roasted Vegetables. See the recipe for Roasted Indian Cauliflower Vegetable Medley on p. 157.)

How to Start If You Feel Overwhelmed

If you're not accustomed to cooking daily, if you eat out a lot during the week, if you're a takeout person, or if this all just seems too much, start slow. Maybe cooking three days a week is too much for you at the beginning. If that's the case, just pick one day a week when you will double or triple your recipe when you cook. Make one batch of vegetables to keep in the refrigerator for the week.

Just work on building the habit of cooking extras. Make a commitment to yourself to do the Gourmet Done Skinny Meal Method at least once a week for a month. Watch the extra meals build in your freezer. You'll love the results, and before long, you'll be using the method three times a week.

If you feel like you're going to need more support on your food-prep journey, don't worry; I've got you covered. Be sure to access the bonus page at gourmetdoneskinny.com/power-of-food-prep-bonus-form to get the goodies. You'll also find information about my Food Prep for Foodies membership group, where I teach live classes on how to use the equipment and how to practice the method. You can find the membership at gourmetdoneskinny.com/food-prep-for-foodies-membership

CHAPTER 5:

Why Do We Rebel Against Food Prep?

We often rebel because we get overwhelmed with the whole idea and think food prep is going to take too much time. Really, it can be super simple if you let it. You don't need to have one big cooking day if you don't want to. I've given you two other ways to do it.

We also rebel because sometimes we don't feel like eating what we had planned. But with my method, if you don't feel like having what you planned, or you don't have time, you can just go to your freezer and choose something else. Because you freeze everything in portions, it thaws out quickly.

The best way to get yourself to prep is to shift away from thinking of it as a chore. So many times, we expect things to be hard, time-consuming, boring, and negative. Make a conscious mind shift to positive thoughts, like "Food-prepping makes my life easier. It's healthier for me, and it eases my stress." Think of food prep as another form of self-care.

In Cookie Rosenblum's Freedom Group we talk a lot about self-care. Think about how you want to feel after prepping your food. Empowered?

Less stressed? In charge of your life? These are all thoughts and feelings that come to mind when I have my food prepped. I've been doing this a long time, and it's not as hard as you might think. But food prep needs to become a positive habit in your life and something you look forward to doing for yourself.

The easiest way to make this a habit is to consistently do Step 1 (choose your meals) on a certain day of the week. That sets you up for the week. But you don't have to plan and write out every meal for every day. Choose your meals according to your schedule. Plan to make three meals a week and to eat leftovers or out of the freezer the rest of the week. Because everything is portioned, you can go to your freezer right before dinner, pull out your portions, and have everything ready in a matter of minutes. Think of it like ordering from HelloFresh or Blue Apron. You have everything to make the meals, so when you go to make dinner that night, take out and create the meal that sounds good.

Of course, some people love to plan every meal for a month, put it on the calendar, and create a big grocery list. This is not me. Although I've done that, I find that food often goes to waste because I don't feel like eating it, or I don't get around to making it like I planned. This traditional way of meal planning doesn't always work when you're trying to eat like a natural eater with intuitive eating, either.

Maybe your mindset is: "I don't have time to cook. I don't like to cook." Well, it's all about your attitude. Let's make it fun. Begin with the end in mind. Think about how great you'll feel when the food is in your freezer. This is the positive mindset of food prep and planning. Prepare for the fun experience of cooking. Instead of a chore, you can make it relaxing by expecting it to be. It's easier than you think. If you change your thoughts, you change your feelings about it. Plan for it. Look forward to it.

My mom is a great example of someone who made a mindset shift. She never enjoyed cooking when I was growing up. In fact, she often said, "I hate cooking." She's seventy-six this year, and she's falling in love with cooking for the first time in her life. She now loves my Gourmet Done Skinny Meal Method of cooking and preserving extras for later. She enjoys going to her freezer and picking out what's for dinner on the days she doesn't have time or doesn't want to cook. Before, it was such a stress, but she changed her mindset, and now she actually looks forward to it. If she can change her mindset after all these years, so can you.

Think of cooking as an experience or a ritual. Set the scene before you start to create an experience you're looking forward to. Think about all the benefits you're going to reap: your health, the delicious gourmet meals lining your freezer, and the time you'll save later. Look forward to the outcomes and benefits of what you're doing. You get ten times your cooking rewards when you think about them ahead of time.

Making breakfast has become an act of celebration and honor for me. My favorite breakfast is my Veggie Skillet Scramble (See recipe on my website). I first make a pot of tea and pour myself a cup. I gather all the vegetables from the refrigerator and grab my favorite knife. Then I methodically cut everything and add it all to the skillet. I chop one piece of bacon, cutting off all the visible and easily removed fat. I peel a garlic clove, use my garlic rocker to smash it, and take a baby spoon and scrape it into the mix. I don't like leftover eggs, so I don't add eggs to my scramble. I'll save what I don't eat at breakfast and have it for a snack later in the day.

When the scramble is almost done, I slice off a piece of my homemade easy bucket bread, which I bake every few days, and put it in the toaster oven on broil for three minutes. (recipe at Gourmetdoneskinny.com/recipes/bread/best-stone-ground-whole-wheat-bread-recipe) I transfer my veggie skillet into my favorite Polish pottery pasta bowl, add my piece of bread to the side, and take it all over the to the kitchen table with my cup of tea. I slowly eat my breakfast while reading email. When I skip this routine, I realize how much I miss it.

So imagine this. You finish work, it's only 5:00 p.m., and you actually have thirty minutes to make dinner tonight. You've chosen Korean Beef as one of your three meals to make this week. (See recipe on p. 115.) You put on some Don Henley and pour yourself a glass of wine.

Next you grab your favorite chopping knife. While listening to your favorite song, you happily chop away at the onions and throw them in the Instant Pot along with some oil, garlic, and fresh ginger. While they are sautéing, you take a sip of wine. Then you mix the soy sauce, brown sugar, some red pepper flakes, rice vinegar, and sriracha together in a small bowl. Next you add the ground beef to the pot, brown it a bit, pour in the soy sauce mixture, and set the Instant Pot to pressure on high for five minutes. Dinner is almost done.

While waiting for the beef to finish, you take a few more sips of wine and savor the wonderful smell of sautéed ginger escaping from the Instant Pot. Now you're ready to start the serving process. You chop some cabbage, shred some carrots, and pull a pack of frozen rice from the freezer and heat it in the microwave. When the beef is done, you place everything in serving bowls on the counter and let everyone make their own Korean Beef Bowls. They choose cabbage, carrots, or rice for a base, topped with the meat mixture, and finished off with a little chopped green onion and more sriracha sauce. Everyone is amazed at your dinner.

After dinner you take the leftover beef and place it in one-cup portions in vacuum-sealed bags, seal them, and store them in the freezer for another time. Or you put the leftovers in containers (I use the black food-prep boxes) in the fridge, labeled with a sticky note that reads "Korean

Beef, Eat by Friday." Or if you're too tired, you have your kids pack it or you do it the next day. You have options. Just be sure to freeze your food by day four after you make it. You now have two extra, beautiful meals in the freezer for another time. How do you feel?

Falling Off the Wagon: Yo-Yo Meal Planning

I'm guilty of falling off the wagon with my eating habits, cooking, food prep, and even exercise a few times a year. I'm bored with what I have in the freezer, or I eat too much over the holidays and vacation and fall back into bad habits. This is usually a lack of self-care, and it all seems to go downhill at the same time. The weather gets bad, so I quit walking every day. I could use the treadmill, or the "dreadmill," when the weather is bad, but I really have to force myself because I would much rather walk outside.

That lack of daily routine sets me up for other bad habits, and I begin to use food as a reward again. I think, *I deserve to eat out and eat whatever I want.* I start treating myself to lunch or dinner out too often. The number on the scale starts creeping up.

Luckily, I recognize this pattern in myself, and I know what to do about it. Been there a million times, and I know I need to focus on why I'm eating out. Most of the time, it's not about food prep. It's about "rewarding" myself with food. So I go back and listen to my old lessons from the Freedom Group.

The trick to getting back on the wagon is to catch yourself as quickly as you can when you find yourself in that situation. Ask yourself some questions. *Why am I doing this? Is it the lack of time to prep?* (For me, lack of time isn't the issue.) *Am I bored with my recipes? Do I need some new ones? Are my habits taking me in the wrong direction, away from what I want in life?* Really dig in and examine why you're not food-prepping anymore.

Many times, you might say to yourself, "I quit doing food prep because I don't have time," when it's really about your lack of focus. Look at your habits. Are you unconsciously living day to day, just trying to get through the week? Did you get out of the habit of choosing your three meals for the week? Think about all the stress it causes when you don't plan out your three meals. Is it really worth it? And look where eating out, ordering takeout, and delivery get you: more calories, more expenses, and feeling unhealthy. Is that worth it? Is this the direction you want to go in?

Of course, things happen. Life gets crazy. You're out of town with a sick family member for a few weeks or something happens at work or at home, and you quit food planning for a while. If it's just for a little bit, chances are you'll have enough food in your freezer to hold out for a while, and it won't be a big deal.

But if you find yourself going back to your old ways—treating yourself and eating out or getting takeout because you're stressed and making excuses, like "I just don't have time," eating bigger portions, and doing it all the time—you've fallen off the wagon. It's time to climb back on.

Try to remember how you felt when you were doing the Gourmet Done Skinny Meal Method consistently. You felt empowered. You felt strong. You were taking charge of your family's health. You were treating your body with kindness, and your body repaid you by feeling energized, healthy, and good. And you were saving money.

Compare that feeling to how you feel now: bloated, lethargic, unmotivated, and heavy. You're gaining weight because you've returned to your old behavior. Hopefully, that mental comparison will get you back on track in a hurry. All it takes is a mind switch; you've done it before, and you can do it again. Think of those wonderful benefits and how food prep makes your life so much easier.

Chapter 6:

Set Yourself Up for Success—Tips and Tricks

The best way to set yourself up for success is to be prepared. You can't cook efficiently if you don't have the right tools. I don't know how many times I've stressed this to my family and friends. For some reason, people think they can use "whatever" in the kitchen. But just like an artist, a plumber, or a woodworker, you need the right tools. They make all the difference. Truly, they do. So before you begin to cook, there are a handful of things you should get and things you can do to make life easier.

What to Get: Helpful Tools and Gadgets

Good knives: This is a must. It's too hard to chop with dull knives. Buy the best knives you can afford; you'll thank me later. You don't even need a full set. My favorites are from Zwilling: a seven-inch rocking Santoku knife, a five-inch Santoku knife, a serrated five-inch utility knife, a small paring knife, and a serrated bread knife. These are the knives I use the most. When I travel, I always take three knives with me: the rocking Santoku, the five-inch Santoku, and a serrated knife. I love cooking for everyone, but I can't stand using bad knives, so they always go with me. I can do pretty much anything with those three knives.

My three favorite knives.

I recently bought my parents the rocking Santoku knife. My mom said the other day, "I just love that knife. It's so easy to chop vegetables." She likes chopping now. Who wants to chop vegetables with a dull knife? It's not fun; it's frustrating. No wonder you hate to food-prep. Get yourself a good knife, and see how fun and mesmerizing chopping can be.

Vacuum sealer: Buy a vacuum sealer. It doesn't need to be fancy; a simple one works well. I like the Anova brand, but the FoodSaver brand is fine too. You don't need all the fancy options, just one that has vacuum seal and pulse options. The pulse option comes in handy when sealing moist foods.

Vacuum-sealer bags: Buy vacuum-sealer bags already made for you. I buy the pint-size and quart-size bags but use the pint-size most of the time. You can buy the rolls to make your own bag and pick your own size, but it's so much faster and easier to have the bags premade. I can't stress this enough. You think you've got time to make your own bags, but believe me, it makes a huge difference when they're the same size and already made. Check the resource section for the bags I use.

Cutting boards: You need a few cutting boards when you're doing food prep. I like the plastic ones with the handle on the end so you can hold the board and scrape a knife against it to quickly and easily move the vegetables to the pan. For cutting raw meat, I use a red plastic cutting board, which helps me remember not to use that board to cut vegetables for salads after I've cut the raw meat. I also use my unique wooden cutting boards, made by my husband, for vegetables sometimes; these also work well when serving charcuterie.

Pans: You need a good stainless-steel skillet so you can caramelize onions. I also like a nonstick pan for cooking and sautéing vegetables because you don't need to use much oil or butter.

Instant Pot: Depending on the size of your family, and if you like to make bigger portions to freeze, I would recommend an eight-quart Instant Pot. The Instant Pot has a million different functions, but when making food-prep recipes, I tend to use the sauté and the pressure cook features the most. The Instant Pot is quite different from a Crockpot. While the Instant Pot does have a slow cooker feature, it's a pressure cooker. It cooks foods like meat, lentils, and beans especially fast.

Containers: Buy same-size containers for storing leftovers in the refrigerator. They can be glass, plastic, or whatever you choose. Rectangle shape works best. I like to use the black food-prep boxes you can often find at Costco because they stack well and stay nice and neat in your refrigerator. You can microwave in them, but I don't typically microwave in plastic. I usually just dish out what I need and microwave the meal in another dish. You'll find the containers I use in the resource section.

Souper Cubes: Souper Cubes are a brilliant idea. You can buy them in all different portions. The ones I tend to use the most are the 1-cup and ½-cup trays. You can find them in the resource section. If you have ever tried to thaw a huge portion of soup in a hurry, you'll appreciate how great freezing your soup in portions can be.

What to Do

Make a commitment to yourself to stick to the Gourmet Done Skinny Meal Method for at least a month. This is important. Building new healthy habits takes time. Make a date with yourself on the calendar to plan your three meals to cook for the week (or at least one meal you multiply for the week). Try to keep your planning date consistent. If you use this method for a month, you'll be rewarded with a variety of meals to choose from in your freezer at the end of the month.

Clean the kitchen. You can't start cooking if your workspace is a mess. It's a lot of work to clean the kitchen first and then make the meal. I realize there are times when you're too tired to do the dishes after dinner. If that's the case, at least rinse them off and put the silverware in a glass of water. The next morning before you go to work, load the dishes in the dishwasher. That way when you get home, your work area is clean. Who wants to start cooking in a dirty kitchen? No one.

Make a list of meals you want to keep in your rotation. Browse the recipes at the end of this book, check out my website, and look at Pinterest. Ask your family to share their favorites. Have these recipes handy when you plan your three meals for the week. You could even print them out, put them in plastic sleeves, and keep them in a binder. When deciding what meals you're making for the week, you could use sticky-note tabs: Monday, Wednesday, Friday. If you need to change the day, no worries; just move the sticky note to another day. Sometimes just having a list to refer to simplifies the whole planning issue.

Put on music or a TV show, podcast, or something inspirational that makes you feel good. I also like silence, depending on my mood. Sometimes I just need some quiet time, and listening to the sound of chopping vegetables mesmerizes me.

Pour a glass of wine or a cup of coffee or tea, and grab snacks. What you choose here depends on the time of day. If I'm cooking in the morning, then I like a nice hot cup of loose-leaf black tea, but around 5:00 in the evening, I like a nice glass of Cabernet.

Create a "Grab and Go" drawer in your freezer. I created this drawer of single-size portions when I was going to be out of town for a while and wanted my kids to be able to grab something quick to eat. I put vacuum-sealed leftovers in a freezer drawer in the house fridge. I labeled the drawer "Grab and Go."

You never know what you might find in this drawer. It might contain a few pieces of frozen lasagna, frozen packets of leftover steak or ribs, a few hamburgers, and maybe a few packets of one-cup portions of soup or rice. This can save you a ton of money on DoorDash or Uber Eats. The other night I was alone for dinner and decided to go digging in the "Grab and Go" drawer. I found some Mexican pork I made a few months ago. I had some leftover rice in the fridge, so I put the pork over the rice, added an avocado and some salsa, and dinner was done.

Other Helpful Hints

Follow the five-day rule. I have a five-day rule for food. Whatever I cook, I eat the dish within five days or freeze within four days. If I pull a portion out of the freezer, then I eat that portion the same or next day. This five-day rule does not apply to fish or seafood. I'm very picky about my them, so I buy and eat them on the same day. You can freeze fish, but I choose not to because I like it fresh.

Label, label, label. I can't stress this enough. You think you know what's in the bag or container, but after it's frozen, everything starts to look the same. If you can't see it, you won't eat it. Make sure boxes of leftovers in the refrigerator have the label on the side facing out when you put them in the refrigerator. That way everyone can see it, knows what it is, and knows when to eat it. I use 2-inch x 1.5-inch sticky notes to label the boxes with what's inside and when refrigerated items need to be eaten, for example, Chicken Cordon Bleu, eat by Friday.

With the label, everyone knows what's in there and when it needs to be eaten. My kids love having choices in the fridge. But if the box gets turned around and it's just a black box, that's the kiss of death. No one even opens it. To label the vacuum-sealed bags, use a permanent marker. Be sure to label the bag before you put the food in. Otherwise, the marker doesn't write as well. I also write the date on the vacuum-sealed bag before placing it in the freezer. In my opinion it's best to eat it within a year for best taste, but technically it won't hurt you if you eat it after that. It just won't taste as good.

Freeze leftover artisan bread in packets of two or three slices. Do you ever buy that good cheese bread from Costco? Or any good artisan bread for that matter? Somehow you never eat it all. A few slices are always left over, get hard, and end up thrown out. When I come home from the store, I take out the bread we need for the next two days, and then I freeze the rest into packages of two or three slices. When we want some good bread to go with our homemade chicken noodle soup, I thaw out a few pieces and toast it. Because it's vacuum sealed, the bread stays nice and fresh. This is a great way to keep a variety of bread choices in your freezer.

Freeze leftover rice, quinoa, or faro. Vacuum seal and freeze leftover cooked grains in flat packets of one-cup portions. These come in handy when you need less than a full pot of rice, quinoa, or faro. Place in a bowl, add a little water when you heat it again if it seems dry, cover with plastic wrap, and heat.

Keep Homemade Chipotle Seasoning on hand. (See recipe on p. 105.) I make a huge batch of this spice blend. It goes great on everything—eggs, vegetables, chicken, pork, and beef. You can even blend it in light sour cream for a quick dip. Having this seasoning handy saves you from pulling all the different spices together when you're preparing the meal.

Refrigerate guacamole and green avocados. Some people keep unripe avocados in the freezer, but I don't recommend that because of changes to the texture and flavor. Keep green avocados in the fridge instead. Take out an avocado a few days before you want to eat it, and let it ripen on the counter. If you only use half, then vacuum seal the other half (with the pit) and store in the refrigerator. You'll be amazed how long the cut avocado lasts. Same with guacamole; vacuum seal it and store in the fridge.

Flash-freeze cookie dough. For the purposes of food prep, flash-freezing refers to freezing individual pieces of food separately. The beauty of flash-freezing cookie dough is that you can pull out just a few cookies and bake them in the evening when you need a quick dessert. Let them thaw for about 15 minutes while the oven or toaster oven is heating, and then bake for about 8 minutes. By baking just a few of these small cookies, you aren't tempted to eat the whole batch, which saves you a ton of calories. I'll bake six small cookies in my toaster oven. Everyone gets a nice little treat, and we don't overdo it. When I taught a bonus class in Cookie Rosenblum's Freedom Group, the members really loved this idea.

But How Do I Do It?

Prepping and cooking are one thing, but what about techniques for reheating or for modifying a recipe? And how the heck do you freeze soup without making a mess? Read on.

Flash-freeze cookie dough in small balls for a few hours before vacuum sealing.

Flash-Freezing: You'll read in many of my recipes my recommendation to "flash-freeze." This means placing the portion on a baking sheet lined with parchment paper and freezing uncovered until frozen. One example: place individual meat loaves on a baking sheet, and freeze until firm. Then place in a bag and vacuum seal.

When you flash-freeze first, the items won't stick together later. Flash-freezing is great for balls of cookie dough, pieces of casserole, or servings of lasagna. Instead of freezing the entire lasagna or casserole, wait until it's cooled. Then cut into pieces and flash-freeze. Once frozen, transfer to vacuum-sealer bags. When you're ready to eat, just pull out the number of pieces you think you need, and reheat them. No waste.

Healthier Recipes: There are so many tricks to making a recipe healthier. Depending on the recipe, you can often substitute nonfat Greek yogurt for sour cream. You can add black or pinto beans for more protein and to stretch out the portions. For soups, it's super easy to add more vegetables to stretch the recipe as well as make it healthier.

I also love to use oil sprayers instead of tablespoons of oil. Just a little spray will often do it, especially if you're using a nonstick pan. One of my tricks for using less butter is to use the oil spray, but then right before serving, I add a small teaspoon of butter to the dish. It adds a lot of flavor, and you don't have to cook the entire meal in butter.

Reheating Your Freezer Meals: The way you reheat dishes is very important. If you don't reheat the dish the right way, you won't want to eat it again. When visiting family and friends, I've observed that they often have no idea how to properly reheat meals. They think you just stick the food in the microwave and heat it. No wonder so many people don't like leftovers. There's a better way to do it so the food tastes as fresh, or almost as fresh, as it did the first time. The broiler, microwave, toaster oven, and stove all work well for reheating. But you need to know when to use each one and for what purpose.

Reheating Pizza: If you just microwave pizza and other foods that have a crispy texture, they get hot, but the taste—yuck! You've got a hot pile of dough, meat, and vegetables. Instead, microwave a slice of pizza for about twenty-five seconds, and then put it on a small cookie sheet and broil it in the oven or toaster oven for three minutes. The microwave warms the pizza in the middle, and the toaster oven crisps the outside. If you do both steps, you'll be amazed at the results.

Speaking of pizza, when the kids were at home and we ordered pizza, there was always a fight about which place to order from. The kids and my husband liked one place, and I liked the other. My solution was to order pizza from both places. I would eat a slice of mine, package the rest in one-slice packets, and vacuum seal them for another time. That way, I had my pizza to eat the next time they ordered pizza. While it's not as good as freshly delivered pizza, it's still pretty good when you reheat in the microwave and crisp it in the toaster oven or under the broiler. And it's a great way to save calories because you just eat a slice and save the rest for another time.

Reheating Hamburgers: If you have half a hamburger leftover, take off the bun, and discard any lettuce and tomato. Reheat the hamburger patty in the microwave for twenty-five seconds or so. Place the bun on a cookie sheet and broil it for a few minutes until crisp. Then place the burger back on the bun and broil for another minute. Add a fresh slice of tomato and fresh lettuce, and enjoy.

Reheating Casseroles and Soups: Soups and casseroles are fine reheated in the microwave. Just reheat until hot to the touch. If you have a few portions of soup to reheat, you can always put them in a pot on the stove. Bring almost to a boil, and then reduce heat and simmer until ready to eat.

Reheating Steak: Heat steak in the microwave for about twenty-five seconds or until warm, and then broil in the oven for a few minutes.

Reheating Fries: Broil fries in the oven or toaster oven until crisp again. Leftover fries (not broiled) are also good to throw into veggie scrambles in the morning.

Always freeze soup in small portions to avoid thawing large amounts.

How to Freeze Soup in Portions

Freezing soup in individual portions makes it so easy when you just want a cup of homemade soup. Over the years, I've developed the best ways to do this. It all started with my homemade chicken noodle soup. When my kids were sick at home, I would make them this delicious soup, but whenever I was sick, what did I get? Canned chicken soup. Yuck!

This did not sit well with me, so I began freezing my chicken noodle soup in one-cup portions. Whenever I didn't feel great or I needed a comfort soup, single portions were ready for me in the freezer. At first, I used plastic bags to freeze the soup, but that didn't work well. It was hard to do, and the bags quickly became freezer burned.

Eventually I figured out two easy ways to freeze soup: the Souper Cube method and the vacuum-seal method.

The easiest way to freeze soups, broths, and sauces is to use Souper Cubes.

I just discovered the Souper Cube method a few years ago, and it's my favorite way to freeze soup and broth. Souper Cubes are a brilliant idea. You can buy them in all different portion sizes. For soup, I like the half-cup, one-cup, and two-cup portions best. You can store the soup right in the trays; however, I like to transfer the cubes to vacuum-sealer bags after they are frozen. In my opinion the soup stays fresher longer in the vacuum-sealed bags. It also allows me to use the Souper Cubes for another soup.

Ladle the cooled soup right into the Souper Cubes. Cover with a lid, and freeze. When solid, let the cubes sit out for about ten minutes. Then remove the blocks of soup and transfer to vacuum-sealer bags if desired. To see step-by-step pictures of this process, get your *Power of Food Prep* resources at gourmetdoneskinny.com/power-of-food-prep-resource-form.

You can also use the vacuum-seal method. I have gone through quite a few vacuum sealers over the years. I've had fancy ones and simple ones. Anova is one of my favorites because it's relatively inexpensive and simple to use. Some of the fancy ones are hard to operate, don't last, and are super expensive. Vacuum sealing soup can be kind of tricky, so here's what I suggest.

First, refrigerate your soup overnight. Doing so makes it easier to handle the soup, package it, and freeze it. Label the vacuum-sealed bag with the name of the soup before filling it. Place the bag in a glass measuring cup. Fold the top of the bag down over the lip of the glass, using the cup to cradle the bag. Ladle the soup in another glass measuring cup, and then pour the soup into the bag.

Carefully angle the bag so it doesn't spill the soup. Press "Manual Vacuum" on the sealer and pulse slightly (a few pulses) to remove some of the air. Then manually seal the bag. Do not use "Automatic Vacuum," or you will suck the soup into the sealer. Lay the soup bags flat on a baking sheet and freeze until solid.

Making Your Soups Healthier: The Secret to Defatting Soup and Broth

I freeze all my soups in one-cup portions. Whenever I want soup, or when I have guests, I just go to the freezer and pick a soup. However, regardless of the type of soup I freeze, I want to make sure it's as healthy as possible. That can mean removing the fat that accumulates in the soup or broth prior to freezing. Here's a trick I use to ensure all my soups are as healthy and low fat as possible

It's super easy to take the fat off most soups and broths. Just put the soup or broth in the fridge overnight. The next day, the fat will have risen to the top and will be solid. Skim that part off with a slotted spoon. It's so much easier than trying to use a separator when the soup or broth is warm.

With broth, it's very easy to remove the fat. Because you have already strained the broth, the fat rises easily to the top. Just remove the top layer. With soup, it's a little harder but still very doable. It doesn't matter if you don't get it all; any little bit of fat you remove makes the soup healthier.

Holiday Parties, Unexpected Guests: How to Prep for Large Occasions

Imagine how great it would be to have a party and just pull out some appetizers you made a few months ago. I did this recently. We had an impromptu get-together, but I didn't stress because I had Spicy Lasagna Appetizers (See recipe on my website.) already made in my freezer. I thawed them out slightly and then popped them in the oven fifteen minutes before the guests arrived. Everyone was amazed.

I do enjoy making fresh food for parties. However, if you're having a big event, you may not have enough time to make all the food on the same day of your party. When planning your menu ahead, you can make and freeze the parts you know you'll need and just put them together the day of the party. Just be sure to make dishes you know taste good after being frozen. Often, I'll do this with foods such as enchiladas, turkey sliders, and vegetarian black bean burgers.

When I plan for a party, I make a grand list of everything I want to serve. Then I write down the days of the week. I look at the menu and decide which items can be made ahead of time, how many days ahead I can make them, and which items need to be made the day of the party.

I put the menu items on my calendar so I know what to make when. For example, I can make the cookie dough way ahead of time, flash-freeze it, and then bake the cookies on the day of the party or the day before if I need more time for other things. I do this for all the menu items. Then I look at the week. Is it too much work at the last minute? If it is, I cut menu items and find other recipes I can make ahead of time.

Holiday Leftovers

While visiting my parents recently for a week, I made them a variety of meals. Before I left to go back home, I packaged the leftovers in small portions. Now they have vegetarian meatballs, pork tenderloin, steak, egg rolls, and soup for another time.

Didn't eat all the cranberries at Thanksgiving? Package and freeze them. They'll go great as a side dish later in the year. Just a few tablespoons of cooked cranberries on a plate filled with steak, potatoes, and salad makes a great addition and adds a little pizazz to the meal. My mom told me recently she was out of fruit for breakfast, so she thawed out a package of cranberries and put it over her oatmeal—a clever idea.

How to Lighten a Family Favorite Dish

All my recipes in this book and on my website are already lightened, meaning they have fewer calories than other versions of the same recipe, making them healthier. But sometimes you may want to lighten your own family favorites. I find some dishes can easily be made healthier, while it's best to just eat a very small portion of others.

Here are some of my tips to lighten recipes:

- Scan the recipe ingredients.

- Look for easy substitutions. Can you use ground chicken or turkey instead of beef, or part chicken or turkey instead of all beef?

- Can you use light sour cream or light cream cheese? Can you use yogurt instead of half-and-half or cream? Often, you don't need as much oil as the recipe calls for, so can you cut down on the oil?

- Do you even need meat in the dish?

- Can you substitute zucchini noodles, butternut squash, cauliflower rice, or other vegetables for the rice or pasta base?

- Use oil spray instead of butter or spoonfuls of oil when browning meats.

- Use a nonstick pan to save on butter and oil calories.

- If your dish contains cheese, can you use less and maybe sprinkle it only on top? Or use less sharp cheese instead of more of the mild?

- Can you bulk up the recipe with more veggies? This also makes the dish go further.

- Can you use less sugar or add in some applesauce to replace the sugar?

If you have a favorite dinner recipe you want me to lighten, email me at amy@gourmetdoneskinny.com. I love doing makeovers. Keep in mind some recipes don't lighten well, but I'll let you know if I can't do it.

Desserts

I'm not a big fan of lightening desserts. I don't care to use fat-free or sugar-free substitutes. I find I don't like them, plus I don't believe artificial ingredients are very good for you. Other than reducing the sugar or shrinking the portion size, I often feel it's hard to lighten desserts.

My motto with desserts: I would rather have a "little tiny piece of heaven" (the real thing) than change the entire recipe into something unrecognizable. Thus, the reason you don't see a lot of "healthy" desserts on my website. I prefer to make them mini, and while the calorie count may be high, at least you can plan for a nice splurge. If you are a natural or intuitive eater you can definitely have them. On my website you can find desserts in the "Not So Skinny" section (Gourmetdoneskinny.com/recipes/category/not-so-skinny-recipes).

Here are a few tips for lighter desserts:

- Adjust your portion size by making sweets "mini"—meaning smaller dessert portions—like mini cupcakes or mini scones.
- Use phyllo cups instead of pie crusts and make the desserts individual and small.
- Adjust the sugar if you can. Most of the time, you don't need the amount of sugar called for. You can usually cut the sugar easily by one-quarter. This doesn't work for all desserts, but experiment and see what works for you. If a recipe calls for 1 cup, try using ¾ cup instead.
- Use low-fat or 2-percent milk, light sour cream, and low-fat sweetened condensed milk instead of the full-fat versions.

How to Organize Your Freezer

At minimum, use containers and labels for storing food in the freezer.

With my Gourmet Done Skinny Meal Method, the freezer is your friend. When I was a young mom breastfeeding my younger son, another mother once said to me, "Having breast milk in your freezer is like liquid gold." I'll never forget her telling me that, and boy was she right. It gave me the freedom to go out with my mom and my friends while my husband watched the kids. Having frozen meals in your freezer has the same benefit. It's like storing gold because it gives you the freedom to do other things.

Organization is key to storing frozen foods. There are many ways to organize your freezer and fridge. I have tried many methods in the past, but ultimately, it all depends on what works best for you and your family. The more organized you are, the easier it is to find the food, and the more it gets eaten instead of forgotten. This can be hard if you don't have a lot of space, but try to keep like things together so you can easily find them. Put all the soup packets in one spot, the chicken dishes in another, and so on. Be sure to rotate your food, and use the older frozen foods first.

Here's my ideal method of organizing frozen foods:

- I have a separate upright freezer in the garage for prepared food.
- In the large freezer, I use baskets or plastic bins labeled with categories, like grilled chicken, soup, desserts, and meat.
- I have a small freezer for uncooked meat.
- I often buy one quarter of a cow and pork from the local rancher and store all the unprepared frozen meat in the small freezer.
- My house freezer is for frozen vegetables, the Grab and Go drawer, frozen pesto, frozen jalapeños and adobo chilies, slices of frozen bread, and other things I can pull out in a hurry to go with dinner.

As I was writing the draft for this book, I called my mom one day and asked, "What are you up to today?" She excitedly said, "I'm organizing my freezer. I started yesterday. It's amazing how many goodies are in there. I didn't realize you left us so much at Christmas." Of course, I giggled to myself.

My mom went on. "It's like a banquet. We're eating well this week. I'm finding things I didn't even know we had—your frozen bread dough, grilled chicken, meatballs, pork tenderloin. I'm pretty excited about it. I'm organizing it all into baskets so we know what we have." She made my day.

Do you have to purchase a separate freezer?

An extra freezer isn't necessary, but it is a total game changer. If you have more space, you can be more organized, and you can find the items you need faster. If it's all crammed in a small freezer, you might not see it. It's frustrating, and you won't want to prep a variety of items.

Buying an extra freezer will save you money in the long run, so it's totally worth the cost and space. I recommend an upright freezer, if you can afford it, because it's easier to see all your items in there without digging. But for about $200, you can purchase a chest freezer, which will give you quite a bit of space. Although I think it's worth it to purchase a separate freezer, you can practice my method with only one freezer.

How to Organize Your Refrigerator

My house refrigerator holds all the homemade condiments, store-bought condiments, and fresh veggies. In addition to the included vegetable bins, I put two separate plastic bins in my fridge for vegetables. Produce takes up a lot of space.

Because I use the black food-prep boxes, everything fits neatly into the fridge. I use those boxes to store rice, meals, pasta, cooked vegetables, and more. I always make sure the sticky note is on the outside so when we look in the refrigerator, we know what we have.

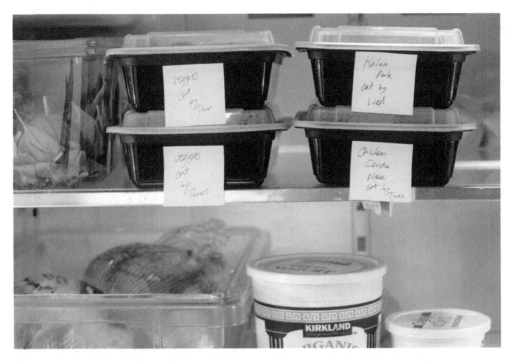

Handy boxes for quick-grab leftovers you'll eat in a few days. Be sure to label them.

When my kids were home and my older son was into bodybuilding and attending fire academy, he would make tons of rice and chicken and store it in the black food-prep boxes. We had stacks of those black boxes in our refrigerator. It's amazing how much one kid can eat. I still think about how much chicken we went through in a week.

Chapter 7:

The Gourmet Done Skinny Meal Method When Traveling

The Gourmet Done Skinny Meal Method comes in super handy when you're traveling somewhere you need or want to cook, like staying in a timeshare with a full kitchen, visiting family, or taking food to family and friends.

I have to admit we're kind of nuts when we go to Aulani Resort in Hawaii. Well, maybe it's just me who's nuts. I've even created a packing list specifically for Hawaii. It includes knives, a cutting board, and my garlic rocker. Because we have a full kitchen, it's so nice to be able to cook breakfast, make some wraps for lunch, and then eat out for dinner. Not only does it save us a lot of money (especially in Hawaii), but it also saves a ton of calories.

Having a full kitchen doesn't mean it comes equipped with pantry items, however. I found that out the hard way the first year we stayed there. We bought a few groceries, like eggs, cheese, and stuff for sandwiches, and the next morning when I got ready to make breakfast, I realized there was no salt or pepper, no oil, and no cooking spray. So I had to be a little creative. I cut up leftover fries, which had oil in them, and a few bites of leftover steak. Then I added vegetables and eggs I had purchased, and I used some salsa I had bought to go with chips. Our Mexican-themed breakfast turned out pretty well.

I now come better prepared. Instead of using oil so things don't stick, I buy bacon; it's great for breakfast and it gives us enough fat to cook anything we need. I bring my own little baggies of kosher salt, black pepper, and Homemade Chipotle Seasoning. Who wants to go out and buy full-size containers of those things and then throw them out when you leave or try to lug them home? You don't need a whole box of salt, just a little.

I also bring extra dishwashing pods because they don't give you enough and extra laundry pods because we hike quite a bit and need to wash clothes more often than the amount of laundry detergent they supply covers. Many people would probably call me cheap, but I call it being practical. I bring two large suitcases: one for me, one for the house stuff. It's kind of like going camping, I guess. I'm not a camper, so this is as close to camping as I get.

In the past, I also brought prepared foods from home, like my Chipotle Egg Cups or frozen grilled chicken. (You'll see how I lugged all this to Hawaii in a minute.) I'll admit, bringing premade food was more important to me back when I was counting calories. Now that I'm a natural eater, it's not as important to me to bring so much prepared food, as I don't need special diet foods anymore. I eat what I want and stop when I'm lightly satisfied.

Now I like to focus on eating different foods from Hawaii and love to visit the farmer's market, which we found by accident, to pick up local produce. Typically, our time in Hawaii was Saturday to Saturday, but one year right before we were getting ready to leave for vacation, there was a big snowstorm in Seattle. They called it Snowmageddon.

The airline called us to see whether we wanted to fly out a day early to get out before the snow. So we did. Adding another day at Aulani at the last minute proved to be ridiculous in price, so we decided to stay the first night in Waikiki, and being downtown turned out great.

The next morning, we took a long walk and ran into a farmer's market—I love farmer's markets. My husband and I split up for a bit, and when he found me, my arms were full of produce. He laughed and said, "What are you planning on cooking? You know we're only going to be here for a week."

Since that trip, I plan our trips Friday to Friday so I can be sure to hit the farmer's market.

These days, I mainly take prepared frozen food only when visiting my parents or in-laws. Because they are getting older, they don't like to cook for company as much anymore. I love to cook for them when I visit. But instead of having to prepare everything when I get there, it's easier to take a lot of my food with me. Plus, they love it, as I often bring things to leave for them later, like frozen soup. My dad loves my homemade chicken noodle soup, and my father-in-law looks forward to my frozen chocolate chip cookie dough already balled and ready to bake.

How to Travel with Prepped Food

The best way I've found to travel with frozen food is to use a soft Yeti cooler. It's made with ColdCell insulation and keeps the food frozen for hours, unlike traditional coolers. I can travel from Seattle to Florida and arrive with still very frozen food.

A good trick to make sure things stay totally frozen is to include a five-pound frozen pork shoulder or another big item in the cooler. It keeps the other frozen foods frozen. When I arrive, I thaw out the pork shoulder and make Kālua Pork out of it (See recipe on p. 111.). This is a Hawaiian dish, not to be confused with Kahlúa, the coffee liqueur.

I put the Yeti in a big suitcase and make sure it's zipped tight. I add a note for security to zip it up tight again if they look in it. I had that issue one time, when they looked inside but didn't zip the cooler all the way afterward. By the time we arrived, the food was only partially frozen. Now I put a note on it that says "Homemade food for parents. Please zip back up tight if you open it. ☺ Thanks!"

The newer Yeti versions use strong magnets instead of the heavy-duty zipper so that might be a better option. Because I travel a lot and have accumulated miles, I can bring three suitcases for free with Delta Airlines, and they are usually pretty generous with their weight allowance.

What to Bring

A lot of what you pack for travel depends on the purpose of your trip. For example, when traveling to Aulani in Hawaii for vacation, I often bring my frozen Chipotle Egg Cups for quick breakfasts, frozen packages of grilled chicken to turn into quick wraps for lunch, and frozen homemade tortillas for the wraps.

What to Take to Family

With my family, it's a bit different. You name it, I bring it. It's a hodge-podge of stuff. I basically clean out my freezer when traveling to visit family. I just fill up the Yeti. I put in all kinds of soup, leftover brisket and steak for my dad, grilled chicken, focaccia bread, veggie meatballs, turkey burgers, pizza dough, bread dough, and a few packets of Parmesan Chicken Broth and Beef Bone Broth (See recipe on p. 139.). I use the broths for cooking and make most of the meals fresh. That way my parents can reap the rewards of the frozen food I brought for them later, after I'm gone.

This year we've rented our timeshare at Disney World for Christmas and plan on having a house full of family. I'll definitely be bringing things to start us out so we don't have to cook the entire time. With twelve to fifteen people, eating out even once a day gets expensive. The great thing is that I can prep food over time before I leave. I don't need to do it all at once. That's the beauty of using vacuum-sealed bags. They keep the food fresh and travel well.

CHAPTER 8:

Break Up the Boredom

If you find yourself getting out of the habit of food-prepping, it may be because you're bored with your meals. To break up the boredom of eating the same things, try some of these great ideas.

When using the Gourmet Done Skinny Meal Method and planning your three meals for the week, think about the seasons, and incorporate seasonal produce. In the spring, for example, I tend to make a lot of amazing salads with all the different lettuces available. Asparagus is great in the spring as well. To make seasonal food prep easier, I've provided seasonal recipes on my website. It's also great to stock up on and freeze seasonal foods, such as berries, to use later. I love making my Berry Cobbler (See recipe on my website.) in January with all the fresh fruit I froze over the summer.

Summer is my favorite season for growing fresh herbs and tomatoes, and I grow about twenty-five tomato plants. If you want to grow tomatoes, the number of plants you need will be determined by the length of the growing season in your area and how many tomatoes you want. I eat tomatoes every day and for almost every meal in the summer. Before summer ends, I make my famous Instant-Pot Homemade Tomato Sauce (See recipe on p. 127.) a few times and vacuum seal it to use in lasagna, pasta dishes, and soups in the fall and winter. It's funny; before I lived in California, I hardly ate tomatoes, but once you've had a Sacramento tomato, you can't get enough of them.

In the fall, I like to incorporate lots of sweet potatoes and a variety of squash, like acorn spaghetti squash, butternut squash, and delicata squash, in my dishes. Delicata is one of my favorite squashes because you can eat the skin, plus it's easy to cut, unlike a lot of squash. I often use squash as a bowl, so we have lots of squash boats with spicy ground turkey or those great fall recipes on my website.

In the winter I make a lot of soups, one-pot meals, bowls, and heavier dishes, like lasagna and meatloaf.

Before the holidays I prep a bunch of meals to help me get through. That way I'm not stressed with all the extra holiday activities. You can check out a helpful post on my website: "10 Healthy Recipes You Need to Make Now Before the Holidays" (Gourmetdoneskinny.com/recipes/breakfast/10-recipes-to-get-you-through-the-holidays-now).

More Boredom Busters

Here are some fun ideas to do with your family to get out of the rut of always cooking the same things.

Photograph Your Meals

Try taking pictures of your meals when you eat out at a restaurant or take pictures of the menus. I do this for inspiration in creating new recipes. It doesn't matter if you don't know exactly what's in the dish. Just make a few notes and be creative when you hit the kitchen. Sometimes a certain ingredient you tried in a restaurant will inspire a totally new creation.

Take a Cooking Class When Traveling

Last year, my younger son and I traveled to Hawaii. Because he hadn't been to Hawaii in a long time, I asked him, "What do you want to do? We can go ziplining, hiking, try a Segway?"

He surprised me and said, "Mom, let's take a Hawaiian cooking class together."

I never would have thought he'd want to do that, and it warmed my heart. So we did take a cooking class. We had a blast, learned how to make traditional Hawaiian food, and then came home and made our own. This is how my Poke Bowl recipe came about. (Find it on my website, Gourmetdoneskinny.com/recipes/main-dish/super-easy-shoyu-poke-bowl) You'll also see pictures of our class and the instructor's pet pig, Bacon.

This year, my sister-in-law, Susan, came with me to Hawaii. Because I had such a great experience with my son in the cooking class the previous year, I signed us up for another cooking class with the same instructor, Chef Linda. This time the class was an Asian infusion class. Again, I had a blast, and Susan did too. It's so much fun learning to cook new foods together.

The instructors make it easy, so even if you think you might feel intimidated, don't worry. They make sure you are successful and have a great time. So when you travel to a new place, check whether they have cooking classes available. I guarantee it adds a new dimension to traveling. If you're in Oahu, check out Hawaiianstylecookingclass.com. Chef Linda is the best.

Take a Food Tour When Traveling

My family and I did a food tour a few years ago in Prague. It was fabulous and opened my eyes to their true food culture. I was interested in the food tour because I had visited Czechoslovakia and the Soviet Union back in the 80s and 90s and wasn't a fan of the food in either place, but I knew I just had to be missing something. I usually love all kinds of food, but I found the Czech food and Russian food bland.

They had to have good food somewhere, so I decided a food tour might be just the thing. And it was. On our Prague food tour, we learned that in the USSR, there was one cookbook for everyone, *Book of Tasty and Healthy Food: Iconic Cookbook of the Soviet Union*, by Anastas Ivanovich Mikoyan. It had over one thousand recipes, with many images and texts showing off the beauty of Soviet life.

Families were expected to cook only from this one book. If Grandma decided to make her famous potatoes one night at dinner, the kids would "turn her in" when they bragged about it at school, and she would get in trouble. Because of that, there was no expression of love with spices or any creativity deviating from the book of recipes. Those things just weren't allowed. Almost thirty years later, on the Prague food tour, we had wonderful food: crispy roasted duck, *knedliky* (bread dumplings), delicious soups, Czech beer, and so much more. I knew they had to have great food. Turns out I was right. But had I not taken the tour, I would never have known that history.

Be Creative with Your Leftovers

Just this morning, my mother called to tell me she'd experimented with her breakfast scramble. My mom loves to follow a recipe, and when she does, she hardly detours from it, so this was a big deal for her.

She had leftover Cajun rice and decided to add it to her skillet scramble with baby potatoes, mushrooms, peppers, and asparagus. She said it was delicious, and my dad loved it as well. It was great to hear the excitement in her voice, as I could tell she was proud of the fact that she created something delicious.

Branch out and be adventurous. You can be creative with any leftovers if you have an onion, mushrooms, crumbled bacon, red peppers, and a little cheese. Don't be afraid to experiment. You never know what you might come up with. Making a meal doesn't have to be complicated.

Often, I create a meal with whatever leftovers I have in my refrigerator, plus items we've purchased at the grocery store. This happens a lot when we visit our timeshare in Hawaii. I love creating breakfast with the leftovers.

After leaving the airport, we head to Costco and the grocery store and stock up on some staples, like eggs, fresh vegetables, fresh pineapple and mango, tortillas, and rice. For breakfast I'll combine restaurant leftovers, such as steak or chicken, with mushrooms, onions, garlic, kale, chopped up French fries, and a little bacon. I turn it all into a Skillet Scramble (See recipe on my website.) for breakfast. Or I'll make a breakfast burrito or rice bowl with the ingredients. Often, I'll make wraps to take for lunch or snack on our daily hiking trips. (I'm not a big fan of leftover fish, so I don't use it in my leftover creations.) It's amazing how much money you can save on vacation by not eating out for every meal.

At home, when I make Kālua Pork (See recipe on p. 111.), I love to make a few different dishes using the leftover pork and Homemade Hoisin Sauce. (See recipe on p. 113.) Together, they make a fabulous pizza. Spread the hoisin sauce on an unbaked crust as a sauce, add some pork, fresh mushrooms, onions, garlic, and finely slice cabbage. Top with a little cheese, and bake. Or you can use the leftover pork to make my Hot Kālua Pig Dip (recipe on website, Gourmetdoneskinny.com/recipes/appetizer/hot-caramelized-onionkalua-pig-dip). Or you can make tacos with the cabbage, hoisin sauce, and pork. Or make a big salad, with spinach, spring mix, fresh mushrooms, pork, and cabbage, and use the hoisin sauce as a dressing. Or a big rice bowl or nachos. One dish used many ways. If you don't want to eat pork all week, freeze it in packs and have the different dishes at another time.

Steak is one of my favorite leftovers. If we have an extra piece, I'll vacuum seal it for another time. When I'm ready to use it, I cut it into tiny pieces, sprinkle it over tortilla chips, add a can of drained black beans, some finely chopped onions, chopped tomatoes, finely chopped jalapeños, black olives, and a small amount of cheddar cheese. Then I broil it for a few minutes in our toaster oven. This is perfect for instant nachos when guests arrive unexpectedly or if I want a quick dinner for two. It's also great over salads, in pasta, and on sandwiches.

If you don't have enough steak, combine what you have with some cooked vegetables to stretch it out. Same goes for leftover chicken. If you just made it, you can vacuum seal it for later. Turn leftover chicken into chicken nachos, put it over a salad or in a wrap, add chopped pieces to pasta with some of my homemade tomato sauce, or make my Open-Faced Creamy Chicken Rainer Sandwich (recipe on my website, Gourmetdoneskinny.com/recipes/recipes/open-faced-creamy-chicken-asparagus-sandwich)

CHAPTER 9:

Mistakes to Avoid

A very long time ago, before I labeled food in the fridge, I had made our favorite pork dish, Cilantro Pork Pot. (See recipe on my website.) At some point, the leftovers from that meal ended up in the back of the fridge. A few weeks later, I made more Cilantro Pork Pot.

One day my son called me at work and asked, "Can I eat the leftover pork?"

"Sure," I said, thinking it was the more recent one and not remembering the other.

Well, he ate the three-week-old pork. He had a bad stomachache, and I called poison control. He was fine, but now he's very picky about outdated food, and we always joke about the poison pork and how I tried to kill him.

We all make mistakes, and after the poison-pork incident, I became much more consistent about labeling. All my food-prep boxes in the refrigerator have sticky notes on the outside of the container, facing out so we can read them.

Avoid These Gourmet Done Skinny Meal Method Goofs

1. Don't freeze roasted veggies. They turn out mushy after you thaw them out and reheat them. Been there, done that. Yuck! Make roasted veggies fresh every week.

2. Don't freeze warm or hot food. Let it cool before freezing. Otherwise, you'll have ice crystals on your food.

3. Don't forget to label food going in the freezer. "Oh, I know what this is. I don't need to label it," used to be my famous last words before adding a dish with no label to the freezer. One day I thawed out salsa, thinking it was chili. Labeling doesn't take much time, and it saves you costly dinner mistakes.

4. Don't fail to label food you're storing in the fridge, and don't allow the prep box to get turned around so you can't see the sticky note. "If you can't see it, you won't eat it." That's my motto. Label the box to identify what it is and when it needs to be eaten by, and make sure everyone can see the label when they open your fridge.

5. Don't freeze shredded cheese. Freezing messes with the texture and makes shredded cheese clump together.

6. Don't freeze cream cheese; it changes the texture. If the cream cheese is in a casserole—not too much of it—it should be okay. Dishes that have a lot of cream cheese do not work well frozen because the consistency changes from creamy to curdled.

7. Don't freeze anything with mayo. It will look normal, but the emulsion will break down and the mayo will have oil floating on the top.

8. Don't cook too much at one time, especially when you're first starting out. Don't plan to cook everything in one day. Make it

> easy on yourself. Make the different parts on different days; then on another day, put it all together.
>
> 9. Don't go to the grocery store without a plan. Not only will you waste time, but you'll waste money too. Plan ahead; it makes a world of difference.
> 10. Don't plan to prep too many meals at once. Plans often change, so stick to three meals at a time. It's doable, and you won't waste food because you can usually fit in three meals a week.

I was recently asked about my failures in the kitchen, and I couldn't think of an example because most of the time I feel like I can fix a mistake by adding something. I rarely throw things directly in the trash if they don't turn out well. Turn your mistakes into new recipes or think of them as feedback for next time. Don't think of them as fatal or failures.

Just the other day, I was listening to an interview with author Bob Proctor, and it dawned on me why I couldn't think of an example of a kitchen failure. He said, "We fail every day. They may be little ones, and we just don't look at them as failures but more as feedback."

When I'm cooking and something doesn't turn out like I wanted, I take notes, and when I cook it again, I "do better next time." I'll add more of something or take away something. But I don't look it as a failure; I look at is as feedback.

If you do have what you think is a disaster, don't stress. Just learn from it. I also believe you can fix anything you've cooked (in the savory department) by adding bacon and cheese. They always makes things better.

I had some learning moments with soup. Before I started using Souper Cubes, I packed my soup and broths in vacuum-sealed bags. It was always a balancing act to hang the bag off the counter and try to seal the bag using the pulse button without sucking up the soup. When I wasn't careful, the soup ended up on the floor. Back then I always waited to mop until after the broth was sealed in the bags and in the freezer. I did figure out a better way, as discussed earlier, to avoid this mishap, but I now prefer the Souper Cubes. They make my life so much easier. Soup on the floor was feedback and helped me figure out a better way.

One of my favorite lessons is, "Don't assume everyone knows what you're talking about." One day, my cousin Angie called me with a question about the Instant Pot. I don't remember exactly what the question was, maybe that she had a "burn" message when she tried to make spaghetti. I just remember being lost about her description of the problem. I just didn't get it. Finally, she sent me a picture. She had put the meal into the Instant Pot, directly on the element without the pot liner, and tried to cook it. Thus, the "burn" message.

I was surprised to hear the pot still worked and she hadn't messed up the element. In Angie's defense, her mom had given her the Instant Pot, and the pot liner ended up stored in the cabinet with her bowls and not in the box with the Instant Pot. She didn't know there was a liner to begin with. I realized then I shouldn't assume everyone knows their way around kitchen appliances and knows what I'm talking about.

Speaking of family disasters, Angie's mother, my aunt, had a doozy as well. I had given her my recipe for bucket bread. (You can find the recipe on the website, Gourmetdoneskinny.com/recipes/bread/best-stone-ground-whole-wheat-bread-recipe.) I had also sent her the vital wheat gluten, one of the important ingredients for the bread recipe, because I wasn't sure she could get it where she lived in Missouri.

My aunt sent me a picture of the bread and told me, "Well it didn't work. It was like rubber." When we dissected the recipe to figure out what she had done, it turned out she'd mistaken the vital wheat gluten for flour and then skipped over adding the gluten called for in the recipe. No wonder it was so rubbery. We had a good laugh over that, and the story of the "rubber bread" disaster still comes up quite often.

FAQs About the Gourmet Done Skinny Method

Why do you use the Instant Pot for many of your recipes? Can I just use a slow cooker?

I use the Instant Pot because it makes my life easier. It's a one-pot method. You can brown meat, sauté, and pressure cook all in one pot. The one pot also goes into the dishwasher, no hand-washing. As a pressure cooker, it also cooks food about thirty percent faster than other methods.

My original Kālua Pig recipe took eighteen hours in the Crockpot on low. It takes seventy minutes in the Instant Pot. Not only is it much faster, but it also tastes even more delicious than cooking it in the slow cooker. Meats turn out tender and juicy when pressure cooked. Instant Pots are great for cooking at higher altitudes as well. No need to adjust times or temperatures.

The beauty of the Instant Pot compared to the old-fashioned pressure cookers is that it is fail-safe. No more dangerous exploding cookers like the ones my grandmothers used.

Unfortunately, you can't use a slow cooker for most of my recipes. Slow cookers deprive the food of oxygen for a long time and give off a stewed taste in my opinion. While many recipes are suited for slow cookers, most of my recipes aren't.

How do I make planning and shopping more doable?

Pick a consistent day of the week to choose your three meals. Try to stick to that day so it becomes a habit. For example, every Sunday morning after I look at my email and messages, I make a list of three meals to make for the week.

Look in your pantry, freezer, and fridge. Make a list of what you need for the recipes. Remember to double or triple the ingredients if you're making more than one batch. If you hate to shop, try using an online service. While it may seem expensive, if you buy over a certain amount, like $35, delivery is often free. Or try the grocery pick-up option. Don't plan to cook on the day you shop.

Is there a way to use less plastic?

Of course. You can always use glass containers instead of the vacuum-sealer bags or the black prep boxes. It's a matter of individual choice whether to use plastic or glass. I hate wasting food. If the food doesn't taste great reheated, I'm not going to eat it and it's going to be wasted. And I believe the vacuum-sealer bags keep the food fresher longer than glass.

The vacuum-sealer bags I use are BPA free. I use these bags for these reasons: 1) they keep the food fresher; 2) it's easier to store them in the freezer; 3) I save money; 4) food lasts longer in vacuum-sealed bags.

Stay up-to-date as I explore other options for environmentally friendly storage processes at Gourmetdoneskinny.com/power-of-food-prep-resource-form

Will this work for me if I'm trying to avoid meat?

There are many vegetarian recipes you can make and freeze, like the Spicy Vegetarian Meatballs and Spicy Black Bean Burgers. (See recipe on p. 163.)

My portion control is out of control. How can your method help?

It's surprising how little food we actually need. Make sure you are eating when you're slightly hungry, not hangry, and only eat until you are lightly satisfied. Pay attention when you're eating. Eat slowly and chew your food carefully. Often, we think we need more food just because it tastes good. Keep asking the question as you're eating, "Am I still hungry?" It takes a good fifteen to twenty minutes after you eat for your brain to register that you're full, so take breaks often to check your hunger level. Also ask yourself, "Why am I still eating this? Is it because I'm hungry or because it tastes good?" If you're still hungry, would a banana suffice? We often eat to soothe our emotions, so pay attention to the why behind your eating.

How about special dietary needs?

Although I can't address the special dietary needs of everyone, and my recipes are for foodies who like and can eat a variety of food, many of my Gourmet Done Skinny Meal Method techniques will work with prepared foods for special diets. If you need special foods in the freezer, you may want to choose prep option B, Batch It. Make one batch at a time and freeze. This is what I do for my mom, who is vegan. I prepare a few dishes for her, portion them, and keep them in the freezer for when she decides to visit.

How do I start simple? I sometimes avoid food prep because I have too many recipe books and too many options.

This is where making a list of your favorite recipes works well. Place those recipes in a binder with plastic-protected pages. You won't be overwhelmed if you've made them before and they're your favorites. If you want to add variety, make only one new recipe per week.

Is there a cookbook you'd recommend as a must-have in the kitchen for novice cooks or for people who don't feel like they cook well?

Most of my recipes are doable even for the novice. I include step-by-step instructions with pictures for all my recipes, and you can always email me questions. I don't really have a basic cookbook I recommend. However if you can find *Complete Step-by-Step Cookbook*, by Better Homes and Gardens, you're in luck. It shows you many special cooking techniques with pictures. It's an old cookbook, but these days you can find out how to do pretty much anything on the internet, or check out my Food Prep for Foodies membership (Gourmetdoneskinny.com/food-prep-for-foodies-membership).

If I can only do this one day a week, will the food keep in the refrigerator? And what's the best way to make pasta or rice taste fresh?

My rule of thumb is to eat everything within five days if you keep it in the refrigerator. If you plan on freezing it, freeze within four days and make sure you freeze it in portions. Rice does get hard if not sealed well in the refrigerator, but you can always add a little water when you reheat it in the microwave. Rice can also be frozen flat in packages. Pasta is harder. It bunches up when refrigerated, so I try to make the amount of pasta I need for the meal. Meals like macaroni and cheese do okay if you add a little milk when you reheat them.

Do you still waste food?

Yes, when I use fresh vegetables and fruits, unfortunately I can't time it all perfectly and it's impossible to not waste some food. Over the years, I've gotten much better about it though. I waste very little prepared food because I try to freeze it before it goes bad. That's one habit I have committed to.

Conclusion

I hope you have enjoyed reading *The Power of Food Prep*. I also hope you've gained a few nuggets of knowledge and I've inspired you to do your own food prep. That's my goal and what I live for—helping others create beautiful meals.

Don't worry if you feel you are not a chef. I'm not a chef either. I wasn't formally trained in food. I just love food and have practiced cooking all my life. As Julia Child said, "You don't have to cook fancy or complicated masterpieces—just good food from fresh ingredients."

You don't have to be a chef; you just have to be someone who loves food and wants to serve your family beautiful, healthy meals every day.

My Gourmet Done Skinny Meal Method has developed over time and has indeed become life-changing for me. This engrained habit has supported and sustained me through some difficult times in my life. Not only has food prep changed the way I eat and what I eat, but I don't really worry about what to eat anymore either. Because I have such a reserve of foods in my freezer, I always have something healthy to eat. That is the Power of Food Prep.

The only time I get a little stressed about food and what to fix is when I visit my family. While I love cooking for them, I'm spoiled with all my freezer staples at home. I love using Homemade Beef Broth and my Chicken Parmesan Broth, so when I visit them, I either need to bring my own in my Yeti cooler or use store-bought versions. I will buy store-bought broth if need be, but the flavor just isn't there.

I'm a foodie at heart. I love having a freezer full of grilled chicken, homemade tortillas, homemade tomato sauce, and homemade pesto. I depend on having these things already made, so it's a pain when I have to start from scratch or buy them already prepared.

Once you start doing your own food prep, you'll be amazed at how spoiled you get. Always having fresh cookie dough in the freezer, so you can bake cookies at a moment's notice when the grandkids come over, will become second nature to you. No longer is it a big deal if people drop by and you decide to serve them dinner at the last minute. No problem. Yep, I'm spoiled. And you will be too. Once you build this habit of food-prepping, it's with you for life.

To quote Julia Child one last time, "I don't think about whether people will remember me or not. I've been an okay person. I've learned a lot. I've taught people a thing or two. That's what's important. Sooner or later the public will forget you, the memory of you will fade. What's important is the individuals you've influenced along the way."

And hopefully I have influenced you with my Gourmet Done Skinny Meal Method.

Don't forget to grab your goodies on my bonus page: gourmetdoneskinny.com/power-of-food-prep-bonus-form

On that page, I have resources for you and a link to my membership. If you want to know more about my Gourmet Done Skinny Meal Method, or if you're unsure about how to put it all together or how to get started on your food-prep journey, check out my membership program.

And now for the recipes.

Recipes

I truly love all the recipes I create, but these are some of my very favorites, which freeze well and are best for food prep. I must admit it was hard to limit myself to just a few.

For step-by-step pictures, videos, nutritional and calorie information, and even more great recipes, visit my website: gourmetdoneskinny.com/power-of-food-prep-resource-form

These are my favorites that I make weekly and keep in the refrigerator to have on hand for the week:

Homemade Chipotle Seasoning—My Large Batch Version

This seasoning blend is so versatile. You can use it to spice up anything. Perfect for steak, chicken, eggs, seafood, dips, dressings, and roasted veggies. Because it's so handy, you want to make a lot at once. Often, it's cheaper to buy the spices in bulk on Amazon, and you can find the chipotle powder on that site.

- 10 tablespoons chipotle powder (Use more or less to taste. This recipe is spicy as it is.)
- 10 tablespoons smoked paprika
- 10 tablespoons ground cumin
- 5 tablespoons kosher salt
- 5 tablespoons garlic powder
- 3 ½ tablespoons oregano
- 3 ½ tablespoons ground coriander

Mix all ingredients together in a medium bowl. Store in an airtight container. I like to use an old Costco-size spice container.

On the Go! Crustless Chipotle Egg Cups

These are one of my favorite foods to food-prep because they make such a quick breakfast. I routinely make a batch or two of these, flash-freeze them on a cookie sheet, and transfer to vacuum-sealed bags in my freezer. They are packed with protein and goodness. One thing to note, use silicone muffin pans, and the egg cups will pop right out. Otherwise you'll spend too much time cleaning metal tins even if you spray them heavily. Just making a batch of these egg cups will save you a ton of money and calories if you're a person who grabs egg bites at Starbucks.

- nonstick cooking spray
- 3 cloves garlic
- ¼ cup onion
- 6 ounces ham

- ½ jalapeño
- 20 whole eggs
- ½ teaspoon kosher salt
- black pepper to taste
- 1 tablespoon of my Homemade Chipotle Seasoning (See recipe on p. 105.) (or use whatever you like)
- 12 tablespoons crumbled bacon (I like to use the Kirkland brand from Costco.)
- 4 ounces reduced-fat cheddar, shredded (about 1 cup shredded)

1. Preheat oven to 350 degrees. Spray silicone muffin cups (2 sets of 12) with cooking spray and place cups on a cookie sheet.
2. In a food processor (or chop by hand), combine garlic, onion, ham, and jalapeño. Lightly pulse until finely chopped.
3. In a large mixing bowl, combine above mixture with the eggs, salt and pepper, chipotle seasoning, and bacon. I like to use my Nutrimill Artiste Mixer.
4. Scoop about ¼ cup of egg mixture into each cup. Try to get a little of the good stuff at the bottom of the bowl for each egg cup. Distribute the shredded cheese evenly over each one.
5. Bake 18 to 30 minutes until set. You don't want them overdone, and every oven is different. If you use a convection oven, bake time is about 18 minutes, whereas a regular oven may take up to 30 minutes. Take the egg cups out once they no longer jiggle when you gently shake the pan.
6. Allow egg cups to sit 5 minutes.
7. Carefully remove each egg cup with two forks on either side. If necessary, run a knife around each cup to loosen before removing. Transfer to a plate or wire rack to cool. When cool,

transfer to a cookie sheet and place in the freezer, uncovered. Flash-freeze for at least 10 to 20 minutes and seal in vacuum-sealer bags.

8. When ready to eat, place egg cup on a plate and microwave for about 1 minute, 15 seconds. All microwaves differ, so test yours to find the best time.

Instant-Pot Kālua Pig

No one will ever know you didn't spend hours on this delicious Kālua Pork done in the Instant Pot. This is a perfect crowd-pleaser, especially when served with my Homemade Hoisin Sauce. (Recipe follows.) Use it in tacos, on pizza, on sandwiches, in lettuce wraps, or over salad greens with a bit of the hoisin sauce for the dressing. This is my go-to when I need something quick and have a lot of guests coming over.

- 1 teaspoon vegetable oil
- 3 pounds pork shoulder roast
- 2½ teaspoons kosher salt or coarse salt
- ½ cup water
- 1 to 2 tablespoons liquid smoke to taste
- 5 cloves garlic
- 5 tablespoons bacon crumbles (optional)

- Serve pork with Homemade Hoisin Sauce (Recipe follows.)

1. Turn Instant Pot on to Sauté. Add oil to pot.
2. Cut meat into three or four big pieces. Sprinkle with salt. Brown meat on all sides. Turn pot off.
3. Add water, liquid smoke, garlic, and bacon.
4. Press "Manual" or on some models "Pressure Cook," and set for 70 minutes on high pressure with vent sealed. Allow pressure to release naturally. If pork is not tender, cook for 10 more minutes.

NOTES

For a 5-pound roast, cook in Instant Pot for 90 minutes. I highly recommend serving this with my hoisin sauce. It's just not the same without it.

Homemade Hoisin Sauce

You'll love this creamy sauce. It's great in lettuce wraps, as a sauce for my Kālua Pig, and even as a dressing. One tablespoon goes a long way and adds a ton of flavor. You can also freeze the sauce in packets to use later.

- 8 tablespoons soy sauce
- 4 tablespoons peanut butter
- 2 tablespoons honey
- 4 teaspoons rice wine vinegar
- 2 garlic cloves, finely minced
- 4 teaspoons sesame oil

- 4 teaspoons sriracha sauce
- ⅛ teaspoon black pepper

Place everything in a container and use an immersion blender to mix and chop it all. (If you don't have an immersion blender, I recommend getting one.) You can also mix in a food processor or even mix it in a bowl if you mince the garlic. I like to just throw it all into my container and then use the immersion blender, and it's done in a flash.

Healthy Instant-Pot Korean Beef

This delicious, quick, easy, healthy Korean Beef is made in the Instant Pot or wok and served over shredded kale, carrots, and cabbage. It's a great family-pleaser and a low-carb option for those watching their carbs and calories. For those not watching carbs, it's also great over rice.

I've been making Korean Beef for years. My boys can't seem to get enough of it, probably because my original version was mostly ground beef, a little green onion, white rice, and no veggies. Times have changed, and I've updated this version and now call it Healthy Instant-Pot Korean Beef.

In this healthy version, I use less brown sugar and have added some vegetables for bulk. I also love to serve it over finely shredded vegetables instead of rice. Leftover Korean Beef is great in scrambled eggs, tacos, and wraps. And you can freeze it.

- ⅔ cup low-sodium soy sauce
- 3 tablespoons brown sugar
- 1 to 2 teaspoons red pepper flakes, depending on how spicy you like it
- 2 tablespoons rice wine vinegar or mirin
- ½ to 2 tablespoons gochujang or sriracha
- 1 teaspoon sesame oil
- olive oil spray (or sesame oil in an oil mister)
- 1 medium sweet or yellow onion, finely chopped
- 8 garlic cloves, minced
- 4 teaspoons ginger, grated fresh
- 2 pounds 90%-lean ground beef (if less than 90% lean, drain fat after browning) or substitute ground turkey or chicken

1. In a small bowl or liquid measuring cup, combine soy sauce, brown sugar, red pepper flakes, rice vinegar, Gochujang, and sesame oil. Set aside.
2. Spray Instant Pot liner with oil from oil mister.
3. Sauté onion, garlic, and fresh ginger for about two minutes.
4. Add ground beef and sauté until most of the beef is browned. Pour in soy sauce mixture.
5. Push "Manual" and set to 5 minutes on high pressure with vent closed.
6. Release pressure immediately when done.
7. Serve over rice, shredded carrots, shredded cucumbers, or shredded kale, and garnish with chopped green onions.

Stove Top Directions: To make this Korean Beef on the stove, use a wok or frying pan. Follow directions to sauté onions, garlic, and fresh ginger for about two minutes. Add the ground beef and cook until most of it is browned. Add the sauce. Cover with a lid and let simmer for at least 10 to 15 minutes, stirring occasionally.

Even Better Than Granny's Meatloaf

Growing up, we never had meatloaf at home because my mom didn't like to make it, so I always ate a ton of it at my grandmother's house. Her recipe wasn't so healthy, however, so I lightened this one many years ago by using half ground beef and half ground turkey. I also added kale for a little fiber. My uncle loves this meatloaf and he's definitely a beef person—he raised cattle. Of course, he doesn't know I snuck some turkey in it.

- oil spray (If you have a good nonstick skillet, no spray is needed.)
- 1½ cups finely chopped red onions (about two onions)
- 1 cup finely chopped celery (about three ribs)
- 2 cloves garlic, minced
- 1 pound ground beef (Use 85 percent lean, not the 93 percent lean, or the meatloaf will be too dry.)

- 1½ pounds ground turkey (I use the 93% lean.)
- 2 eggs, beaten
- 2 tablespoons Homemade Chipotle Seasoning (See recipe on p. 105.) (You can use less. It's not super spicy but has a nice kick.)
- 2 teaspoons salt
- 2 teaspoons black pepper
- 1 tablespoon Worcestershire sauce
- ⅔ cup ketchup, divided
- 1 cup old-fashioned oatmeal, uncooked
- ¾ (stalk removed) finely chopped cup kale (A food processor works well.)
- 12 tablespoons crumbled bacon bits (I like the Kirkland brand from Costco.)

1. Preheat oven to 350 degrees.
2. Spray a large nonstick skillet with oil if necessary. Heat stove to medium temperature. Sauté onions, celery, and garlic until soft.
3. In a large mixing bowl, combine ground beef, turkey, eggs, cooked vegetables, Chipotle Seasoning, salt and pepper, Worcestershire sauce, ⅓ cup ketchup, oatmeal, and kale.
4. Using a dry measuring cup (¾ cup), scoop out the meat mixture, form a loaf, and place into a mini nonstick loaf pan. Repeat until done with 12 loaves. (My mini loaf pans are a set of 8, so I use 2 pans and have 4 empty loaf spaces, which I then fill with water. This makes them bake more evenly). If you use muffin pans or individual casserole dishes, you may have to adjust the bake time.

5. Spoon remaining ketchup over each loaf (almost 1 teaspoon per loaf) and top with 1 tablespoon crumbled bacon. Press bacon down into meatloaf slightly so it doesn't fall off when baking.

6. Bake loaves until internal temperature reaches 165 degrees, about 25 minutes. When finished baking, carefully lift out each loaf with a spatula and fork and transfer to a wire rack or serve immediately. Allowing the loaves to sit in the juices will soak up the extra grease. You don't want those extra calories.

Best Healthy Grilled Chicken Recipe

The secret to this easy, perfectly moist and delicious grilled chicken recipe is in the brine. No need to marinate. You won't believe how simple this healthy grilled chicken is. Just brine, sprinkle with seasoning, and grill. And don't be scared away by brining, there's nothing to it.

This recipe came about because of my husband. He's the grill master in the house, and it was his idea to brine the chicken and grill it on our Traeger grill. Originally, he just used whatever spice mix we had on hand. Later, we started using my Homemade Chipotle Seasoning (See recipe on p. 105.) which is the best grilled chicken seasoning in my opinion.

Brine
- 1 cup kosher salt
- 3 quarts water

- 1 large pack of chicken thighs or breasts, about 7½ pounds
- Homemade Chipotle Seasoning or any other spice you want to use (e.g. Cajun)

To Brine the Chicken

1. In a big plastic container with a lid, or in a bowl, mix the salt and water. Add chicken. Cover with lid or plastic wrap.
2. Allow to brine overnight or at least 1 hour in the refrigerator. Overnight is best.

To Grill the Chicken

1. Preheat grill to 375 degrees. You can use gas, charcoal, Big Green Egg, Traeger, or whatever grill you have.
2. When the grill is hot, remove chicken from brine and lay chicken flat on the grill. Try to spread the pieces out. You may have to do this in a few batches.
3. Sprinkle generously with Homemade Chipotle Seasoning or whatever seasoning you're using.
4. Grill chicken for about 15 minutes. Flip over and grill until the internal temperature reaches 165 degrees (about 10 minutes more).
5. Remove chicken from grill and allow to cool. Then cut into bite-size pieces, and freeze in vacuum-sealed bags. I like to freeze them in 1-cup packets. Use this in wraps, over salad, over pasta, and in tacos.

Creamy Instant-Pot 40-Clove Garlic Chicken

This Creamy Instant Pot 40-Clove Garlic Chicken is comfort food at its best, and it's super easy to make and clean up! You can serve it over brown rice, cauliflower rice, or even eat it alone. Leftovers freeze well. This is the perfect one-pot meal.

- 1 tablespoon olive oil, or use olive oil spray
- 8 chicken thighs, boneless and skinless
- 1 onion, finely chopped
- 40 cloves garlic (I buy peeled garlic at Costco for this. It's much easier.)
- 1 teaspoon kosher salt
- ¼ cup sherry
- ½ cup chicken broth or my Parmesan Chicken Broth (See recipe on my website.)

- 8 ounces fresh mushrooms, chopped (optional)
- 1 15-ounce can cannellini beans, drained
- 2 sprigs each rosemary and thyme, finely chopped
- 4 ounces light cream cheese

1. Press "Sauté," Add olive oil or spray. Heat Instant Pot.
2. Add 4 chicken thighs, brown for about 5 minutes, and then flip over and cook the other side. Remove chicken to a plate. Repeat this for the second batch. Remove all chicken.
3. Add chopped onions to the Instant Pot, and add more oil if needed. Brown onions for about 5 minutes, stirring occasionally. Add in whole garlic cloves. Cook for another minute.
4. Add in sherry and chicken broth. Cook for another minute.
5. Put the chicken back in the Instant Pot, and add the mushrooms, beans, and herbs. Press "Manual" and pressure cook on high for 10 minutes. Allow to natural release for 10 minutes.
6. Stir in light cream cheese. Serve over cauliflower rice, brown rice, or zucchini noodles.

Instant-Pot Homemade Tomato Sauce—No Peeling, Coring, or Seeding

While I love my quick cherry tomato sauces, I also enjoy making a sauce with fresh plum tomatoes, such as San Marzano tomatoes, which takes longer. Normally I'll simmer the sauce for hours on the stove after having spent a lot of time peeling, coring, and seeding the tomatoes first.

One year after buying a fifteen-pound box of San Marzanos (because I didn't grow enough), I decided it was time to figure out how to make my homemade sauce in the Instant Pot. I had a few things in mind before creating the recipe.

I didn't want to peel, core, or seed the tomatoes. Although seeded sauce gives you an extraordinary taste, it takes a lot of time. I also feel like I'm wasting most of the tomato because very little is left after peeling, coring, and seeding. Additionally, it requires lots of tomatoes.

I really wanted to do it in the Instant Pot because I didn't want to stir it all day. This sauce also needed to have great flavor without a ton of calories. I wanted a healthy tomato sauce free of added sugar and without a lot of oil.

My Instant-Pot Homemade Tomato Sauce fits all three of my criteria. I used sweet onions and baby carrots instead of sugar. I used fresh herbs, garlic, plum tomatoes, and a Parmesan rind to add flavor. See what you think. It really doesn't take much prep time; most of the time is spent pressure cooking and simmering. You do need an Instant Pot, and an immersion blender is also super helpful. In fact, if you don't have an immersion blender yet, this might be the recipe that changes your mind.

How do you make this sauce and how can you use this sauce?

I hope you like my Instant-Pot Homemade Tomato Sauce. I make several batches and freeze them in two-cup portions in vacuum-sealed packages. When I need tomato sauce, I microwave it until slightly thawed and add it to my pot. This sauce is a basic sauce, meaning you can add your own spices and season it the way you want in your dishes. It's great in lasagna or spaghetti sauce, over vegetables, and with other pasta. Thicken it with some tomato paste, and you'll have a great pizza sauce as well. It's very versatile.

- 4 tablespoons olive oil (Use a good brand.)
- 3 large sweet onions, (such as Maui, Vidalia, Bermuda, Walla Walla, or Sweet Imperial), sliced and roughly chopped
- 1 cup baby carrots, roughly chopped
- 10 garlic cloves, minced
- ½ cup water

- 6 pounds San Marzano tomatoes, Roma, or any other plum tomato
- ⅓ cup finely chopped fresh basil
- ⅓ cup finely chopped fresh parsley
- ⅓ cup finely chopped fresh oregano
- ½ cup red wine (Cabernet works well.)
- 1 tablespoon kosher salt
- 1 Parmesan rind, about a 2-ounce piece (See note at bottom of recipe.)

1. Press the "Sauté" button on your Instant Pot and heat. Make sure to press the "Adjust" button and set sauté on the highest setting. Later in the recipe, you'll switch it to low, but for now, you need the highest setting.
2. When hot, add the olive oil.
3. Add onions and sauté until softened and slightly brown, about 10 minutes.
4. Add carrots and garlic to the pot, and sauté a few more minutes. Be careful not to burn the garlic, or it will be bitter.
5. Add water and whole tomatoes. If you have a 6-quart Instant Pot, you'll probably need to cut a few of your tomatoes so they all fit in the pot. If you have an 8-quart, you should be fine. Mix the onions and tomatoes as best you can.
6. Cover with lid. Press "Manual" (or "Pressure Cook" on some models), and make sure it's on high pressure. Set time to 20 minutes. If your pressure cooker won't pressurize, add another ½ cup water. Usually there's enough liquid with the ½ cup water, tomatoes, and onions to pressurize, but if not, add a bit more.

7. When finished, do a quick release (natural is fine too). Add basil, parsley, oregano, red wine, and salt. Use an immersion blender to blend all the ingredients into a nice, smooth sauce. Be careful, as the sauce is hot. If you don't have an immersion blender, carefully put the tomatoes in a food processor, in batches, and process until smooth. Put the sauce back in the Instant Pot.

8. Add the Parmesan rind. Push the "Sauté" button and adjust it to the lowest setting. Simmer for about an hour (lid off), stirring occasionally. Try not to let it boil.

9. Taste and adjust spices as needed. (You can also do this last bit of simmering in a big pot on the stove). Remove rind.

10. Cool (I let sit overnight in the refrigerator), and then pack vacuum-sealed bags or Ziploc bags of 1 or 2 cups of sauce.

NOTES

Many times, you can find Parmesan rinds at the grocery store. Just ask at the deli and cheese counter. Otherwise buy a small piece of Parmesan and cut off the rind yourself.

An immersion blender is pretty critical in this recipe. It saves you time and effort by blending the hot tomatoes and onions right in the Instant Pot without making a mess.

I tried using dried oregano, but it seems all wrong in this recipe. I really like the taste of fresh herbs. If you do use dried, go easy, a little at a time, and taste between additions.

Easy Instant-Pot Gourmet Chicken Cordon Bleu

I love Chicken Cordon Bleu, but I wanted an easy and quick recipe that brought all the creamy, cheesy, chicken-ham-and-broccoli goodness together. Thus, this delicious and quick recipe was born. Serve over butternut squash spirals, zucchini noodles, or pasta. This is definitely a family-pleaser.

- 2 teaspoons oil or oil spray (I like to use my olive oil mister.)
- 1 cup finely chopped red onion (I chop the onions and garlic together in my food processor.)

- 2 cloves of garlic, minced
- 1½ pounds boneless skinless chicken breast, cut in bite-size pieces
- 1½ cups cooked and cubed ham steak
- 4 cups chopped broccoli
- 1 tablespoon finely chopped fresh rosemary
- 2 tablespoons sherry
- 1 tablespoon Worcestershire sauce
- 1 teaspoon salt
- ½ teaspoon black pepper
- ½ cup chicken broth or water
- 4 ounces ⅓-reduced fat cream cheese, cut into chunks
- 4 ounces Swiss cheese, grated
- ¼ cup grated Parmesan cheese
- 1 tablespoon corn starch, if needed

1. Serve over butternut squash noodles, zucchini noodles, cauliflower rice, or white or brown rice.
2. Press "Sauté" on your Instant Pot.
3. Add 2 teaspoons oil along with a bit of oil from your Misto sprayer.
4. Add onions and garlic and cook for about 2 minutes, stirring occasionally and spraying a bit more oil, if needed.
5. Add chicken and cook for about 1 minute. Turn off Instant Pot.
6. Add ham, broccoli, rosemary, sherry, Worcestershire sauce, salt, pepper, and chicken broth. Stir.
7. Set the cream cheese on top of the mixture, but do not stir it in.
8. Cover Instant Pot with lid and set to seal. Push "Manual," or on some models, "Pressure Cook," and set for 3 minutes. Yes, really,

3 minutes. It takes a while for the Instant Pot to heat up, so by the time the 3 minutes are up, the chicken is cooked perfectly.

9. When time is up, do the "Quick" release and open the pot.

10. Stir in Swiss cheese and Parmesan cheese. If they don't melt completely, push the "Sauté" button and stir until mostly melted. If you want it a bit thicker, place about ¼ cup sauce mixture in a cup, add 1 tablespoon cornstarch, stir well, and put back into Instant Pot. Cook until thicker. (This sauce also thickens after cooling.)

11. Serve immediately over butternut squash noodles, zucchini noodles, or pasta. (See note at bottom for noodle directions.)

NOTES

Use a spiralizer to cut the butternut squash or zucchini noodles. To cook the butternut squash noodles, spray a nonstick skillet with oil, toss in noodles, and sauté until tender. If using zucchini noodles, only sauté until barely tender, otherwise they become too mushy.

On the older Instant Pot models, you can just use ¼ cup water or broth, but the newer models will give you a "burn" notice, so use ½ cup.

Healthy Air-Fryer Popcorn Chicken

This Popcorn Chicken makes a great appetizer and a fabulous fried chicken salad when topped with my Skinny Blue Cheese dressing.

- 8 ounces light cream cheese, softened
- 1 egg
- 1 lemon or lime, cut in half and squeezed
- 3 tablespoons Homemade Chipotle Seasoning (See recipe on p. 105.), divided
- 2 pounds boneless, skinless chicken thighs or breasts, fat trimmed, cut into bite size pieces
- 2 cups flour
- 1 tablespoon kosher salt
- black pepper to taste
- 1 tablespoon smoked paprika
- ½ cup skim milk
- olive oil spray

Skinny Blue Cheese Dressing, or any other dipping sauce (optional). (See recipe on my website).

1. In a large bowl, combine softened cream cheese, egg, lemon or lime juice, and 1 tablespoon of homemade chipotle seasoning. Use a hand mixer if desired.

2. Stir in chicken pieces. Allow to marinate at least 30 minutes, or even overnight, in the refrigerator.

3. In a large Ziploc bag, add flour, two tablespoons of chipotle seasoning, kosher salt, pepper to taste, and paprika.

4. Preheat air fryer to 375 degrees.

5. Add a few pieces of chicken to bag and shake. Place chicken on a baking sheet lined with parchment paper.

6. Do this for all the chicken pieces. (At this point you could air fry now, but the chicken wouldn't be as crispy. It's best to coat it twice. You can also decide to splurge and deep fry; it's fine to deep fry at this stage).

7. When finished breading all the pieces, dip the coated pieces in milk and back into flour mixture again for a second breading.

8. When you have enough ready for one batch, place chicken in air fryer, spray well with olive oil, and air fry for about 8 minutes. Flip over if necessary and spray again. Air fry another 5 to 7 minutes. If you have the Breville Smart Oven Air Fryer, or a similar air fryer, you won't need to turn your pieces over. (Times are approximate. Each air fryer is different. Watch carefully on a small batch so you know when to take them out.)

9. Total air frying time is about 12 to 15 minutes, depending on your air fryer. Be sure to serve hot.

NOTES

I've learned a few things after making this recipe a million times. First, don't batter the chicken pieces until you are ready to fry, otherwise you will have to re-batter them. The flour soaks into the chicken, and it won't be as crispy if you bread them too long before frying. Second, shake off any excess flour before air frying, and third, spray the pieces well with the olive oil spray. Finally, serve immediately. The chicken loses its crispiness if you try to keep it warm in the oven.

The popcorn chicken freezes and reheats well. Flash-freeze on a baking sheet; then transfer to vacuumed-sealed bags. To reheat, bake for about 10 minutes at 350 degrees or until hot.

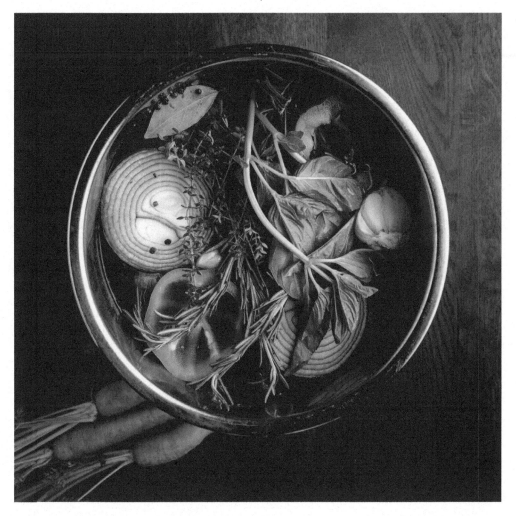

Healthy Instant-Pot Beef Bone Broth

Although I have been making broth for years on the stove, I recently decided I wanted to be able to do it quicker using the Instant Pot. I did some research first so I could create for you the best recipe possible. However, after researching a ton of recipes, my head was spinning from all the different information and opinions.

Varying Opinions

For some bone broth recipes, you throw it all in the pot and go. Others blanch and roast before cooking, and still others blanch, roast, pressure cook, add veggies, and then pressure cook some more. Some experts say you shouldn't add vegetables; some say you should. The list of varying opinions goes on and on. I even read about how the bone broth made in the Instant Pot isn't as good as the broth you simmer for forty-eight hours on the stove. After reading all the information and opinions, I felt crazy. I was even sorry for a while that I researched anything. But after a few weeks of letting ideas percolate in my head, I went to work in my kitchen. I made and tested many batches of bone broth, using my own ideas and some ideas I thought were relevant.

So what method is best?

For me, it comes down to time. Even though I love taking my time on recipes, forty-eight hours of cooking and leaving the stove on overnight is not for me. My family loves beef, but we don't need our house to smell of it for days, nor do we want to take a chance and burn the house down.

So this is my best recipe for Instant-Pot beef bone broth, which I will be using from now on. If I have some time, I will blanch, roast, and then pressure cook. If I don't have as much time, then I just roast and pressure cook. I do feel roasting makes a huge difference, enough to justify the extra time, so I suggest you don't leave out that step.

Why would you even want to make your own broth? Why not just buy it at the store?

Flavor, flavor, flavor. Homemade broth makes your food taste like a chef made it. It does take some time, but it's not hard and you can freeze your broth for later use. There are no preservatives and less sodium. You have total control.

It's also healthy for you. Bone broth has been reported to boost immunity, fight the common cold, fight inflammation, strengthen bones and teeth, and even promote weight loss. All of that in a cup of bone broth. Interesting enough, the benefits of bone broth sound very similar to the benefits of drinking tea.

What are the differences between stock, broth, bone broth, and consommé?

Stock is very concentrated because it's made with lots of bones and simmered for hours, sometimes days, on the stove. It's primarily used as a base for soups, stews, and sauces. A good stock is viscous from the breakdown of collagen in the bones and cartilage and should gel when chilled. Stock is lightly seasoned.

Broth is a more of a soup in itself. It's lighter, less gelatinous, and is often more highly seasoned. Vegetables are often added in addition to the bones. It's sometimes made only with meat, no bones.

Bone broth is essentially stock, but it's not as concentrated. It became popular a few years ago with the Paleo diet, and bone broth sounds catchier than bone stock. My beef bone broth recipe is a combination of both stock and broth. It's thinner than typical stock and not as gelatinous, but it's lightly seasoned. I do this on purpose so it's more versatile. You can add it to almost anything and then add your own seasoning to your dish.

Consommé is basically clear beef stock. It's gently simmered with a mixture of lightly whipped egg whites and lean ground meat. The egg whites and meat congeal and act as a raft, collecting all protein particles and leaving the stock clear. That is not this recipe.

Where do I get the bones? What kind should I buy?

You can buy bones (most often frozen) at small butcher shops, some grocery stores, and even online. I often get mine from Skagit River Ranch, where I buy a quarter cow every year. They just throw them in with my order. You can also save your own bones from your cuts of meat, but I don't often have too many bones, as I buy most of my meat boneless. As to what kind to buy, I like to add a mixture of beef, pork, lamb, and oxtail, essentially, whatever I can find. I think a mixture tastes best for broth. No need to stick to one kind. I also add one chicken foot if I can find it. It gives the broth a good mouth feel.

Why and how do you blanch bones before making stock or broth? Do I have to do it?

Blanching gets rid of any impurities that give your broth an off flavor. It also makes a clearer broth. And it's easy. Basically, you just add your bones to a pot. Cover with cold water and boil for twenty minutes. That's it. You will see scum and foam rise to the top—those are the impurities. Just skim them off. Remove the bones when done and proceed to roasting.

Of course, there are different opinions on the need for blanching. Depending on the bones, the impurities removed with blanching could negatively affect the flavor of the broth. My rule of thumb: if I have time, I blanch, if not, I don't. I have made many broths without blanching and they turned out just fine, no unusual flavor.

Should I roast the bones first?

Yes, roasting the bones matters. It adds tons of rich flavor, so it's worth the forty-five minutes of roasting time.

What is the purpose of using vinegar, and why does it need to sit?

Vinegar helps extract the minerals from the bones. Be sure to allow the bones to sit in cold water with vinegar before you heat up your Instant Pot. If the bones are hot, the pores are closed, and the minerals can't be extracted. Although some say to let it sit for an hour or two, because the Instant Pot takes some time to warm, I think at least thirty minutes is fine.

And don't worry; you won't taste the vinegar if you use an apple cider vinegar. White vinegar is too strong.

What vegetables should I add to my bone broth?

You can add almost any vegetables or vegetable scraps, but stay away from broccoli, cauliflower, Brussels sprouts, and hot chilies. They can overpower your broth and make it taste bitter. Some people save veggie scraps and put them in the freezer. When they get a bag full of scraps, they make broth. No need to waste time and cut them up fine; rough cut is great as you will strain it all anyway.

Cooling your finished broth is important. After your bone broth is finished, strain it and pour it into two containers so it cools faster. Bacteria grows very fast if the broth is left to cool as an entire pot in the refrigerator, so you want to cool it as quickly as possible. The next day, skim the fat off the top and then package it in one- and two-cup vacuum-sealed bags or Souper Cubes and pop them in the freezer for later use.

To Make Healthy Instant-Pot Beef Bone Broth

- 3 pounds assorted beef bones
- 1 chicken foot (optional)
- 1 celery stalk, rough cut in big pieces
- 1 onion, skin on, cut in ½
- 3 carrots, rough cut in a few pieces
- 1 head of garlic, skin on cut in ½
- 2-inch piece of ginger, rough cut
- 1 tablespoon kosher salt
- 2 tablespoons black peppercorns
- 2 bay leaves

- assorted whole fresh herbs (I like to use rosemary, thyme, basil, sage, and parsley.)
- 3 tablespoons apple cider vinegar
- about 8 cups water, or more, filling Instant Pot almost to max line

1. Preheat oven to 425 degrees.
2. Place the bones on a baking sheet and roast for 45 minutes, until brown.
3. Place hot bones (carefully) in Instant Pot. Add bits of brown scraps from baking sheet, if there are any, but leave the grease.
4. Add remaining ingredients and fill Instant Pot to almost max with cold water.
5. Allow to sit for at least thirty minutes; an hour is best. The vinegar will help extract the minerals from the bones.
6. Cover with lid. Set to "Sealing" (in older models).
7. Press "Manual" or "Pressure Cook" and set time to 180 minutes. If your Instant Pot doesn't go to 180, do 120; it will be fine. My 6-quart doesn't go that high, so I do 120 if I make the broth in that size pot.
8. When finished, allow to naturally release. Divide into two pans so the broth will cool faster. If your broth doesn't make 10 cups, add ice. You could add water to get to the 10 cups, but adding ice cools is faster. If you want a stronger broth, make less than 10 cups.
9. Cool in refrigerator overnight. This allows a thin layer of fat to rise to the top, and you can easily skim it off. If you don't mind the fat, you can use it right away.
10. The next day, skim the layer of fat and throw it away. Put broth in vacuum-sealed bags and freeze flat until needed. Or try the Souper Cubes.

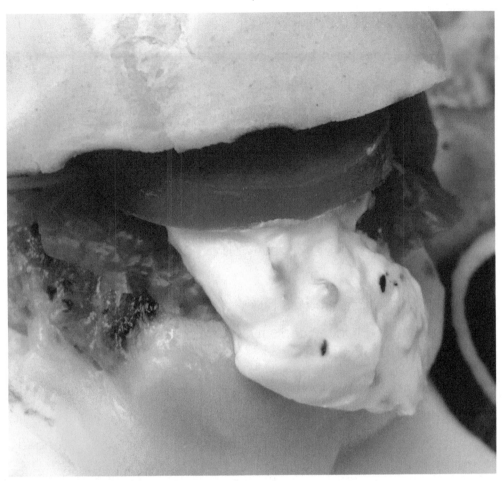

Scrumptious Turkey Sliders - Really!

These turkey sliders are so delicious no one suspects they are healthy. This recipe makes a big batch. Store in the refrigerator for a few days or flash-freeze for about thirty minutes; then transfer to vacuum-sealed bags to have on hand when you want a quick lunch or dinner.

- 1 teaspoon butter
- ½ large sweet onion, finely chopped (about 1 cup)
- 4 cloves garlic, minced
- 3 pounds ground turkey (93% lean)
- ½ cup Italian breadcrumbs

- 1 teaspoon kosher salt
- ½ teaspoon ground black pepper
- 1 tablespoon Worcestershire sauce
- 1 teaspoon liquid smoke
- 1 teaspoon soy sauce
- 2 tablespoons whiskey (yes, really!)
- 1 egg, beaten

   flour just enough to coat the burgers
- olive oil spray (I like to use my olive oil mister.)

1. If you have time, add the butter to a nonstick skillet and sauté the onion and garlic on medium heat. If not, just use the raw onion and garlic.
2. In a large mixing bowl (I do this as I'm waiting for the onion and garlic to brown) combine all ingredients except the flour. Add the browned onion and garlic mixture. Mix well with spoon or hands.
3. To make them uniform in size, use a ¼-cup dry measuring cup to scoop out the turkey mixture. Tap gently in your hand to get the meat out of the cup and transfer the mound to a cookie sheet with parchment paper. Do this for all turkey mounds. You should get about twenty-four.
4. Allow them to chill for about twenty minutes. Then shape gently into patties.
5. Lightly press an indentation in the middle of each slider. This prevents them from puffing up when grilled. Dip them lightly in flour. This forms a light crust on the burger.
6. Preheat the grill to medium-high heat. Then spray the grill heavily with oil from olive oil sprayer so the burgers will not stick.

7. Cook for about 5 minutes. Then lightly spray each burger with oil before you flip them over. Carefully flip the burgers and continue cooking until done (about 5 more minutes). It's important to cook the burgers to at least 165 degrees. You want them done, but you don't want the temperature much more than that, or they will be dry.

8. These freeze extremely well.

Homemade Jalapeño Bacon Cheddar Mini Scones

These delicious homemade scones go great with salad, chili, or soup. Make them now, eat a few, and freeze the rest for later.

- 3 cups all-purpose flour (or if you have self-rising flour use that and skip the baking powder and salt), plus an extra ¼ cup for hands and cutting board
- 1½ tablespoons baking powder
- 1 teaspoon Homemade Chipotle Seasoning (See recipe on p. 105.)
- ¾ teaspoon salt
- ½ teaspoon black pepper
- 8 tablespoons cold unsalted butter
- ½ cup shredded sharp cheddar
- ½ cup chopped jalapeños, (about 3 jalapeños)

- 12 tablespoons crumbled bacon (I like to use the Costco Kirkland bacon crumbles.)
- 2 garlic cloves, minced
- 1½ cup low-fat buttermilk, divided

1. Preheat oven to 400 degrees.
2. Line baking sheets with parchment paper.
3. In a large bowl, combine 3 cups flour (lightly spoon flour into dry measuring cup, do not pack), baking powder, Homemade Chipotle Seasoning, salt, and pepper.
4. Cut butter into small cubes. Add to flour mixture. Cut in with a fork or pastry blender.
5. Add cheese, jalapeños, bacon, and garlic. Mix well.
6. Add 1 cup buttermilk. Lightly fold until most of the buttermilk is absorbed. You don't want to stir hard, just lightly keep folding over, otherwise the scones will be tough.
7. Scoop about 1 cup dough, from the part that is well moistened, into a dry measuring cup.
8. Lightly flour your hands and board. Dump the cup of dough into your hands and make a ball. You will probably have to push the dough together to keep it from falling apart. Lightly press the ball of dough down on a floured board until you have a round disc about 5 inches in diameter. Round the edges with your hands. Cut the disc into 8 pie-shaped pieces.
9. Carefully transfer each scone onto a parchment-lined baking sheet, allowing a few inches between scones. Do this for the rest of dough, adding the remaining ½ cup buttermilk to moisten the flour mixture at the bottom of bowl. (See note.)
10. Bake for about 8 minutes. These do not get very brown.

11. Allow to cool on baking sheet. Eat some and freeze the rest for another time.

NOTES

I've found it better to add the buttermilk in parts as you go. I first add one cup of buttermilk then scoop out the moistened part and make a few scones. Then I go back, add a little more buttermilk, and scoop out the rest.

If you add all the buttermilk at once, the top will be sticky and the bottom of the mixture will be dry. If you try and mix it all together, it will be a big mess and your scones will be tough. Use the dry measuring cup to measure your dough; that way your scones will all be an even size. You will probably have to free form the last bits of dough into scones.

If you need to add a bit more buttermilk, go ahead. Just don't make the scone mixture sticky. Make sure your butter is cold and your oven is preheated and hot. This will make the scones rise better.

To freeze, let scones completely cool. Then seal in vacuumed seal bags. I usually put four in a pint size bag. To reheat frozen scones, place in foil and reheat at 350 degrees until hot.

Skinny Blue Cheese Dip

Looking for an easy, healthy, and delicious blue cheese dressing recipe? This homemade blue cheese dressing with Greek yogurt is simply the best. It has only four ingredients, and it makes a perfect dip too. It's also a great topping to replace mayonnaise or ketchup on the turkey sliders.

- 10 ounces non-fat, plain Greek yogurt (about 1 ¼ cups)
- 5 ounces blue cheese or Gorgonzola crumbles
- 2 garlic cloves, minced (I like to use a garlic rocker.)
- 1 tablespoon Champagne vinegar
- fresh ground black pepper to taste
- 1 to 2 tablespoons 2% milk (Use skim milk if you want it thinner.), (optional)

Mix all ingredients in a small bowl with a fork, mashing the blue cheese into the yogurt. I like mine thick, but you can thin it with a bit of milk if you want it thinner. This keeps for about two weeks in the refrigerator.

Spicy Roasted Vegetables

These spicy roasted vegetables are so easy to make, take little time, and keep you full all day. You can vary the vegetables, depending on what is in season. If you don't like them spicy, leave out the chipotle seasoning and jalapeño. I make a big batch on Sundays to have them throughout the week.

This is my go-to snack of choice. I also add them to salads along with some chicken for protein and use them on homemade pizza or as a side dish for dinner. They go great with a tablespoon of my Homemade Hoisin Sauce. (See recipe on p. 113.)

- 1 lb package baby carrots, whole
- 1 large onion, red or sweet, cut in 2-inch chunks
- 1 jalapeño, finely chopped
- 2 garlic cloves, finely chopped

- 10 garlic cloves, whole (See note.)
- 1 red pepper, chopped into 2-inch chunks
- 1 yellow pepper, chopped into 2-inch chunks
- 2 cups fresh green beans, cut into 2-inch pieces
- 1 zucchini, cut into 2-inch chunks
- 8 to 16 ounces sliced mushrooms (I love mushrooms, so I use a lot.)
- 1 to 2 tablespoons olive oil (Start with 1 tablespoon, and add more if needed.)
- 1 tablespoon Homemade Chipotle Seasoning (See recipe on p. 105.) or whatever seasoning you like
- kosher salt to taste
- black pepper to taste

1. Preheat oven to 425 degrees.
2. In a large bowl (or combine directly in roasting pan) combine all ingredients. Mix well.
3. Place vegetable mixture in a large nonstick roasting pan.
4. Bake for 15 minutes, and then stir well.
5. Bake another 10 to 15 minutes, until carrots are tender when pierced with a fork.

NOTES

To make things easier when I need a lot of garlic cloves, I buy them in bulk, already peeled, from Costco. It's so easy to just toss a handful of garlic cloves into the roasting pan. Don't worry that it will be too garlicky. The garlic mellows when roasted.

Roasted Indian Cauliflower Vegetable Medley

This is one of my rotating vegetable dishes I make every week to have on hand for snacking. It's very versatile. It makes a great filling side dish or snack. Also check out my Indian Chicken Cauliflower Wrap on my website (Gourmetdoneskinny.com/recipes/side-dishes/indian-chicken-cauliflower-wrap-with-cilantro-lime-cream).

- 3 tablespoons sesame oil (or substitute olive or vegetable oil)
- 1 tablespoon ground turmeric
- 1 tablespoon ground cumin
- 1 teaspoon coriander
- 1 tablespoon kosher salt
- 3 garlic cloves, minced
- 2 teaspoons freshly grated ginger
- ¼ teaspoon cayenne pepper (optional)

- 32 ounces cauliflower, chopped into small florets (pre-chopped cauliflower florets, or 1 big head cauliflower)
- ½ jalapeño, finely chopped (optional)
- 1 large potato, diced
- 1 cup frozen or fresh peas

1. Preheat oven to 425 degrees.
2. In a small bowl or glass measuring cup, combine oil, turmeric, cumin, coriander, salt, minced garlic, ginger, and cayenne. Stir well.
3. In a large bowl, combine cauliflower, jalapeño, potato, and peas. Add in oil mixture with spices, and combine well so cauliflower is coated.
4. Spoon mixture into a nonstick 9 x 13-inch baking dish (Spray baking dish with oil if not nonstick). Bake for about 15 minutes, and then stir. Bake for another 10 minutes or until potatoes are cooked through and tender.
5. Serve in bowls as a snack. Top with Tomatillo Green Salsa if desired. (See recipe on my website).

"Clean Out Your Refrigerator" Stir Fry Recipe

This healthy stir fry recipe is made with whatever vegetables and meat you have on hand in your refrigerator. You can use pretty much any protein—beef, chicken, pork, ground turkey, shrimp—and any vegetables. The key to this delicious and easy recipe is the stir fry sauce, my delicious Homemade Hoisin Sauce (See recipe on p. 113.), which brings it all together and makes it taste great.

- 6 cups fresh vegetables (Use a variety of what you have, such as carrots, mushrooms, red or yellow peppers, onions, broccoli, broccolini, snow peas, sugar snap peas, green cabbage, kale, bok choy, radishes, or jalapeños.)
- 1 pound fresh meat, such as top sirloin, chicken thighs or breasts, or pork chops (cut into bite-size pieces), or ground turkey, ground beef, ground pork, or shrimp
- kosher salt to taste

- 2 tablespoons sesame oil or vegetable oil, divided
- 1 tablespoon freshly grated ginger
- 2 garlic cloves, minced
- 3 tablespoons Homemade Hoisin Sauce (or store-bought hoisin sauce)
- 1 to 2 tablespoons sriracha sauce (optional for more spice)
- 2 cups cauliflower rice or rice

1. Cut vegetables into bite-size pieces. I usually put them all together in a big bowl.
2. If not using ground meat, cut the meat into bite-size pieces. Pat with a paper towel to remove excess moisture. Sprinkle lightly with kosher salt.
3. In a large nonstick skillet or wok, heat about 1 tablespoon sesame oil on medium heat until hot.
4. Add meat and cook in batches if needed. Stir fry just until done. (Cook beef until lightly pink). With fattier cuts, drain the grease if needed. Remove from the pan and place on a plate or in a bowl.
5. Add 1 tablespoon sesame oil to wok or pan.
6. Add fresh garlic, ginger, and vegetables. Stir fry for 3 to 8 minutes, until almost tender. (I like mine a little more cooked than raw but not overcooked.)
7. Add Homemade Hoisin Sauce and cooked meat to the pan and heat until everything is hot. Add sriracha sauce if you like it spicier.
8. Serve over cauliflower rice or rice.

Spicy Instant-Pot Pinto Beans

These beans were created especially for Casa M Spice Co®
(Casamspice.com) using their Chain Reaction Spice. They are super
quick to make and are high in protein. Eat them plain or use them in your
favorite Mexican spiced dishes.

- 2 slices center-cut bacon, chopped into 1-inch pieces
  1 medium yellow or white onion, chopped into ½-inch pieces
- 2 cloves garlic, minced
- 2 cups dry pinto beans, washed and any stones removed
- 2 guajillo peppers, seeded and stems removed
- 2 tablespoons Casa M Spice Co (Casamspice.com) Chain
  Reaction seasoning (I like using the uncontrolled version in this
  recipe.)
- 2 teaspoons kosher salt

- 6 cups water
- ¼ teaspoon liquid smoke (optional)
- cilantro or parsley for garnish (optional)

1. Turn on Instant Pot to "Sauté." Add chopped bacon, onion, and garlic. Brown for about 5 minutes.
2. Add beans, guajillo peppers, Chain Reaction spice, kosher salt, water, and liquid smoke (if desired).
3. Set Instant Pot to high pressure for 55 minutes. When it's done, let pressure release naturally or at least allow it to sit 15 minutes before releasing pressure.
4. Serve beans with broth or strain. Garnish with a little cilantro or parsley if desired.

I am a brand ambassador for Casa M Spice Co® (Casamspice.com) because I love their different flavor combinations. All of their spices are low in sodium—about 80% less—with no perceivable loss in flavor.

NOTES

Beans not done? No worries. Just put the lid back on and pressure cook for another 10 minutes. It happens sometimes.

Spicy Vegetarian Meatballs

Even meat-eaters love these veggie meatballs. They're easy to make, and are very tasty. You can serve them over zucchini noodles or pasta with a tomato-based sauce, serve them alone, or turn them into unique appetizers.

- 1 teaspoon olive oil (or use olive oil spray)
- 1 cup finely chopped mushrooms
- 1 red pepper, finely chopped
- 3 cloves garlic, minced
- ½ onion, finely chopped
- 2 15-ounce cans black beans, rinsed and drained well
- 2½ tablespoons Casa M Spice Co® (Casamspice.com) Chain Reaction seasoning
- 1 can green chilies, drained
- ¼ teaspoon liquid smoke (optional)
- 1 teaspoon kosher salt
- 2 tablespoons ketchup

- ¾ cup oatmeal, then finely grind them using food processor
- ¾ cup Parmesan cheese
- 2 eggs

1. Preheat oven to 400 degrees. Spray a large nonstick skillet with olive oil spray or use a teaspoon of oil. Heat on medium heat until hot.
2. Add mushrooms, peppers, garlic, and onion. Sauté for a few minutes until soft.
3. In a food processor, add the well-drained beans, and pulse lightly until partially mashed. Or use a fork to mash the beans.
4. In a large bowl, combine beans, vegetable mixture, Chain Reaction Spice, drained green chiles, liquid smoke, salt, ketchup, oatmeal, Parmesan cheese, and eggs.
5. Using a small 1½-inch scoop or spoon, scoop mixture (to make 1½-inch balls) onto a parchment sheet sprayed with cooking spray or oil.
6. Bake 10 minutes, carefully turn with spatula, and bake another 10 minutes. Flash-freeze on baking sheet, and transfer to vacuum-sealed bags.

About the Author

Amy Lawrence is the CEO of Gourmet Done Skinny, where she empowers foodies and family cooks to rise above mediocre and become masterful in the kitchen. Dedicated to helping families avoid the dread of eating boring, bland meals, Amy is passionate about teaching other foodies how to make healthy gourmet meals to enjoy today, preserve, and freeze for another day.

Her signature Gourmet Done Skinny Meal Method blends the efficiency of meal-planning and prep with the creativity and fun of Amy's signature recipes to create flavorful, satisfying, nutritious meals that make the cook of the house feel like a gourmet chef. The results are less food waste, greater savings on grocery and takeout food bills, noticeable weight loss, and improved efficiency in the kitchen. She has combined her talents and love of cooking to produce healthy gourmet recipes for her company and food blog GourmetDoneSkinny.com.

Amy's love of cooking came from watching her grandmother make homemade noodles in her tiny kitchen. Amy grew up loving food, and started cooking for others at an early age. She has been in the food and tea industry officially since 2003, but she jokes it has been her calling since the day she was born.

As owner and operator of her own tea company for thirteen years, Amy managed a restaurant and tearoom in California and a retail tea shop in Washington state, where she blended her own teas and sold them to retail and wholesale outlets. In 2004, her tearoom won "Best Small Tea Room in the USA."

Amy has taught numerous cooking classes, written more than fourteen books, and produced instructional cooking videos, and she continues to keep up with her weekly recipe blog.

A former special education teacher, Amy extended her love of teaching to the world of food and tea. She has been an instructor for the World Tea Expo and Northwest Tea Festival and a special guest on the *Weight Loss Made Real Podcast*. Amy has also been a featured panelist and speaker for events with noted experts, such as James Norwood Pratt, Roy Fong, Jane Pettigrew, and Cookie Rosenblum. She is a proud member of eWomenNetwork.

Her career shift to food blogging sparked an interest in food photography. Although she considers herself a relative newcomer to the field, Amy often receives compliments from readers and blog visitors regarding her outstanding photographs of her healthy gourmet recipes.

A military brat born in Germany, Amy has lived all over the United States and Germany. She earned a master's degree in special education as well as a bachelor's degree in education and German, all from Kansas State University. While in Germany, she earned an associate degree from the University of Maryland's Munich campus. Amy currently resides in the Pacific Northwest and is building a home in Idaho. She loves to travel with her family and has been all over the world, including visits to China, Russia, Ukraine, Czechoslovakia, Poland, India, and Nepal.

A Day in the Life of Amy

I love my job! It's so varied, and I never get bored because it has so many different and interesting parts. Some days I create recipes, some days I create new posts, and other days I photograph food. Some days I create videos of my recipes; some days I eat out, looking for new inspiration. I often take pictures of menus, so I readily have a list of new recipes and tastes to create and experiment with.

You never know where inspiration will come from. I love eating out on vacation because that seems to be when inspiration hits me the most—like the cooking class in Hawaii with Chef Linda. Or I try a new dish that's super high in calories, and I think, "I could make this recipe over so easily and lighten it."

My usual day is anything but "typical." Because I work for myself, I am in charge of my schedule. While most days I do work at home, there are some days when I do more writing. Then you might find me at Nordstrom Café, having lunch and creating new posts on my computer.

When I'm creating a new recipe, I make notes about what I want and research key words and ingredients I want to use. I start writing the ingredients out as a recipe without amounts on my computer. So it's basically just a list of ingredients. Then I go to the kitchen and start creating. I usually make the recipe three or four times, depending on what it is. Around the second time, I write in the amount of ingredients, and the third time, I adjust them as needed. I also begin writing the directions for the recipe on the second round. The second and third time I make a recipe, I usually photograph the step-by-step directions and final-product photo. The fourth time is usually video creation if I'm doing a video.

After the recipe creation and photography, I edit all the photos. Then I create the post. Many people are frustrated about the length of recipe posts. They want you to "just get to the recipe." What they don't realize is the recipe posts need to be a certain length and have certain keywords so Google picks it up in searches. When you search for "Homemade tomato sauce in the Instant Pot," I want you to see my recipe first on the page. How many times do you click through to the third page of results to get a recipe? Never. So all the writing and keywords in the post help ensure you see my new recipe.

And those annoying ads? Well, that's how we food bloggers get paid. We put all our recipes, pictures, and videos out there for free. All those hours we spend creating, making, photographing, and videoing our recipes is work we give away for free. Those pesky ads provide us income. I know they can be super annoying, but they are our bread and butter, so to speak.

Acknowledgments

This book was a labor of love. So many have contributed to it and provided material and support over the years whether they recognize it or not. While it's hard to thank and acknowledge everyone individually, here goes: my family, especially my parents, Thomas and Barbara Culling; my sons, Thomas and Jacob, and soon-to-be daughter-in-law Hannah; my in-laws, Stan and Michele Lawrence; my sister-in-law, Susan Lawrence; my uncle Ron McClanahan, my aunt Carolyn McClanahan, and my cousin Angie West.

My good friends who have supported me and all my endeavors: Gina Hoskins; Jennifer Goodman; Matt, Katie, and Joe McCord; Vikram Gopel and Vrithi Pushkar, Chris and Masumi Bell.

My mentors: Sandra Yancey, Cookie Rosenblum and her Freedom Group members, Laurie McDermott; my Mastermind Team: Lani Donaldson, Dr. Karen Wilson Starks, Ame-Lia Tamburrini; my Gourmet Done Skinny Private Group members; my Afternoon to Remember tea customers; my beta readers: Michele Lawrence, Susan Nunley, Barbara Culling, Thomas Culling, Gina Hoskins, Tammy Meese, Judy Stephens, Carla Bendo, Brianna Rossi, Lani Donaldson, Kathleen Luttrell, and Jacob Lawrence; the entire Elite Online Publishing team: Anita Henderson, Karin

Crompton, Candice L Davis, Melanie Johnson, Jenn Foster, and all the rest. They are fabulous!

And lastly, my husband, Patrick Lawrence, who encouraged me to write and helped me publish my first book so long ago.

Resources

Books

Tribole, Evelyn. *Intuitive Eating: A Revolutionary Anti-Diet Approach.* Blackstone Publishing, 1995.

Rosenblum, Cookie. *Clearing Your Path to Permanent Weight Loss.* Real Weight Loss for Real Women, 2014.

Kessler, David A., MD, et al. *The End of Overeating: Taking Control of the Insatiable American Appetite.* Simon & Schuster, Inc., 2009.

Articles

Southern Living Editors, "26 Julia Child Quotes That Make Us Love Her Even More," www.southernliving.com/culture/celebrities/julia-child-quotes

"The Link Between Fast Food and Weight Gain," The New York Times, The Times in Plain English, accessed May 28, 2022, www.thetimesinplainenglish.com/the-link-between-fast-food-and-weight-gain

"The Real (Calorie) Cost of Dining Out," Craving Something Healthy, accessed May 28, 2022, cravingsomethinghealthy.com/the-real-calorie-cost-of-dining-out

Link:abcnews.go.com/Health/restaurant-meals-higher-calories-fast-food-studies-find/story?id=19170366

Instruction
Food Prep for Foodies membership group,
Gourmetdoneskinny.com/food-prep-for-foodies-membership

Equipment Resources
Gourmetdoneskinny.com/power-of-food-prep-resource-page/

Made in the USA
Columbia, SC
29 August 2022